D1555176

Ethical Conduct
and the
Professional's Dilemma

ETHICAL CONDUCT AND THE PROFESSIONAL'S DILEMMA

Choosing Between Service and Success

BANKS McDOWELL

Q

QUORUM BOOKS
New York • Westport, Connecticut • London

Library of Congress Cataloging-in-Publication Data

McDowell, Banks
    Ethical conduct and the professional's dilemma : choosing between
service and success / Banks McDowell.
      p.   cm.
    Includes bibliographical references and index.
    ISBN 0–89930–596–2 (alk. paper)
    1. Professional ethics. I. Title.
BJ1725.M36   1991
174—dc20   91–18

British Library Cataloguing in Publication Data is available.

Library of Congress Catalog Card Number: 91–18
ISBN: 0–89330–596–2

First published in 1991

Quorum Books, One Madison Avenue, New York, NY 10010
An imprint of Greenwood Publishing Group, Inc.

Printed in the United States of America

The paper used in this book complies with the
Permanent Paper Standard issued by the National
Information Standards Organization (Z39.48-1984).

10 9 8 7 6 5 4 3 2 1

Copyright Acknowledgments

Contents

Preface

The immediate motivation for the project that led to this book has to be credited to The Center for the Teaching and Study of Applied Ethics at the University of Nebraska. Its call for papers to be presented at a *Conference on Moral Problems in the Professions: Advocacy, Institutional Ethics, and Role Responsibilities* in March of 1990 caused me, for the first time, to think systematically and formally about the problems presented in this book.

The roots of this inquiry, however, reach back into my early teaching career and perhaps even further to my time as a law student. Early in my teaching, students brought me to see that any thoughtful person entering the professions, and perhaps all thinking adults, are faced with a genuine dilemma if they want to be decent and moral, and at the same time aspire to worldly success. Many teachers and other adult "sages" like to proclaim that there is no necessary conflict between these two goals, that it is possible, and perhaps even easy, to be both a moral human being and a worldly success. Young people are rightly suspicious about the ease of that resolution. They often suspect that the tension between these two life goals presents problems they will have to live with their entire professional lives. This book is an effort to explore the context and difficulties of that struggle, both from the individual's viewpoint and the position of society.

The book is written from several perspectives. The first, and for me most important, perspective is that of individual professional practitioners who face the dilemma of choosing right versus success and who must deal with the tensions and real-life choices produced by it. I hope the discussion will make them aware that they are not alone with the problem and will help them better understand the options as well as the difficulties. Awareness alone will not solve the problem, but without it there is little hope of improvement.

A second audience, somewhat different, consists of students entering the profession who bring both idealism and cynicism to their studies. My hope here is to reinforce the former and minimize the latter.

A third audience is made up of professional educators who must be honest and realistic about the professional world into which their students are moving. At the same time, they must strengthen the ethical and idealistic commitments that will help students serve as professionals rather than act as purely profit-driven business people.

Finally, I want to consider the problems from the perspective of the profession as a group or entity. The professions are suffering from serious erosion in the public's traditional perception of them as callings devoted to public service and client-oriented performance. Professionals are increasingly depicted as a group of greedy, self-interested, and often incompetent performers undeserving of special status or income. The professions cannot solve this problem merely through public relations techniques, but must deal with the fundamentals of how professional services are being delivered. Here they need to help individual members by some restructuring of professional roles, by better support of those professionals who are ethical, and by much better policing of incompetent and unethical practitioners.

It is difficult to totally avoid the use of singular descriptive nouns, such as "the professional" and "the client." When necessary and to achieve uniformity and preserve gender fairness, I will designate all singular professionals as female and all singular customers and clients as male, unless that is inconsistent with a particular context. This choice reverses the usual stereotypes.

A great many people and groups have assisted me in this

project. In addition to The Center for the Teaching and Study of Applied Ethics at the University of Nebraska and the host of students who in one way or another kept pushing this problem into my consciousness, I want to particularly thank the following:

Paul Siskind, a senior colleague and later dean at Boston University School of Law, was discussing this dilemma with his students and junior members of the faculty when I was a young teacher there in the early sixties.

Stuart W. Twemlow, M. D., a psychiatrist and friend, led me to see how crucial the mutual decision making of professional and client could be.

The Mid-America Psychosocial Study Group at Menningers in Topeka, in a discussion of a draft, helped me better understand the perspectives of psychotherapists and physicians.

Steven Kalish and Robert Audi, who directed the Conference on Moral Problems in the Professions held at the University of Nebraska at the end of March, 1990, and the participants—particularly the journalists, accountants, engineers, and architects—showed me how the dilemmas facing members of those professions were similar to and different from those of the older professions of law and medicine.

Joel Levin, a former student and now a friend, who combines being a trained philosopher and a successful legal practitioner, did his usual meticulous (I am tempted to say merciless) job of criticizing my language and at the same time made insightful suggestions on that portion of the manuscript he found the time to read.

Bill Rich, a colleague, and Helen Rice, a nursing educator and law student, read drafts and made helpful comments.

My research assistant, KiAnn Dodd, a student at Washburn University School of Law, searched through the libraries and produced much of the information on which this analysis is grounded.

The greatest debt, as always, is owed to my wife, Ellen, whose sympathy sustained me, whose patient rereading of successive manuscripts helped reduce the technical jargon and unclear phraseology, and whose probing criticisms eliminated more than a few errors in judgment.

Ethical Conduct
and the
Professional's Dilemma

1

Introduction: The Dilemma

A great and recurring ethical dilemma facing all professionals (at least at some time) bubbles along under the surface and erupts nastily from time to time into full public view. This is created by a conflict between the two primary roles performed by the same person: the professional as advisor to a client who asks whether certain services are necessary, and the professional as provider of the services the client might need. The steady flow of newspaper articles in recent years charging that surgeons perform unnecessary operations,[1] that stockbrokers churn accounts and act on inside information, that insurance agents sell unsuitable policies to customers, and that lawyers bring frivolous lawsuits shows that this dilemma is often resolved the wrong way.[2]

THE NATURE OF THE DILEMMA

Although all professionals struggle with this dilemma, it helps to have a particular context in which to develop the complexities of the problem, as well as an analysis of possible solutions. As I am a law teacher and most familiar with legal situations, my running example will be the case of a lawyer who is asked to advise a client whether to pursue litigation and who would also be the attorney representing the client in such litigation. If she advises that the probability of recovery is insufficient to justify suit, her charge will be modest, often just for an office visit. If she represents the client in court, her fee will be substantial, many times greater than the cost of advice. A defendant's attorney faces the same problem. If the defense is so weak that there is minimal probability for a favorable verdict, the case should be settled. The client would then be saved litigation costs, the bulk of which would be the defense attorney's fees.[3]

One qualification needs to be made about this example. I use it because it is best for analysis. It is not, however, where the dilemma most often occurs for lawyers in litigation. The problem of unnecessary services does not arise solely in situations where the client needs no service at all. The more common context occurs when some service is necessary, but the professional pads bills by giving excessive service. For the lawyer who has elected to file an action or to defend one on behalf of a client, that can happen from unnecessarily large amounts of trial preparation, such as pursuing exhaustive discovery, filing semifrivolous motions, refusing to stipulate, or delaying settlement long after it is clear that the case will be settled because there is no serious disagreement about what the result should be.

The same general problem faces other professionals, such as a surgeon asked whether an operation is necessary, or a physician asked about the necessity of some treatment. An insurance agent may be asked whether a customer needs more insurance. The stockbroker is often asked about the advisability of an investment.[4] All face essentially the same dilemma and are presented with the same choices. When professionals serving both as counsellor and purveyor of services abuse their position by advising that unnecessary or more expensive services should be purchased, this increases the provider's income, but at the client's cost.[5] Although this dilemma is faced by any provider of services or goods who is asked for advice, it is a particularly difficult one for professionals.[6]

It may seem inappropriate to describe the choice facing the professional as a dilemma. A dilemma is a choice between two alternatives, both of which are or appear unfavorable, if not always equally unpalatable.[7] Here, the choice seems clear and unproblematic. Professionals are obligated to give honest advice on whether services are necessary and to prefer the client's interest over their own. Professionals are also driven by economic necessity and cultural expectations to be financially successful, however. In many situations, the professional perceives herself or may be perceived by other people as having to select one or the other; that is, be ethical and pass up an opportunity to make money, or take advantage of an opportunity and be unethical. Many students in professional schools and many practitioners would say that describing this as a dilemma accurately reflects their feelings. For some, there appears to be no dilemma because they can easily and unequivocally select one or the other of the dilemma's horns; that is, they can either give advice based purely on the client's best interests, or act at every opportunity as "bottom line" profit-makers by enhancing their income. For most professionals, torn in some degree between the two goals, the cost is internal and psychological—strong feelings of conflict and guilt. For the profession as a group, the cost is the appearance of hypocrisy. The profession publicly adopts high ethical expectations to which formal allegiance is given, but practices appear to be at sharp variance. "High ideals often cohabit with venial practices."[8]

There are two contradictory views of professions in contemporary society. One widely held, or at least publicly proclaimed, by professionals themselves is that they are conscientious experts devoted to improving the lot of both society and their clients. Whatever compensation they receive is genuinely earned by the value of their services. Another view, found broadly among members of an increasingly cynical public, is that professionals are a rapacious, greedy, often incompetent lot who are frequently overpaid to do more damage than good.

My starting point is that both views are accurate, or at least contain some truth. The average professional is a typical human being which means a bundle of contradictions, containing within himself or herself the capacity for genuinely virtuous and altruistic activity, as well as the capacity for mean, selfish, and greedy activity. One well-known example is Abe Fortas, the prominent

Washington lawyer, Supreme Court justice, and confidant of Lyndon Johnson. While an enormously successful lawyer in private practice, Fortas performed much dedicated *pro bono*,[9] or charity work. This included representing Owen Lattimore throughout his ordeal of being accused of disloyalty by Senator Joseph McCarthy,[10] and defending Monte Durham in the case that established the Durham rule for insanity defense in criminal cases.[11] His most famous *pro bono* work was the representation of Clarence Earl Gideon before the Supreme Court in *Gideon v. Wainwright*,[12] which produced the important constitutional principle that every criminal defendant, whether he can afford it or not, is entitled to competent legal counsel.[13] Yet this same Abe Fortas was later forced to resign from the Supreme Court for improperly accepting compensation from a potential litigant who might come before him while he was a justice, a matter that raised serious questions of conflict of interest in violation of the Code of Judicial Ethics.[14]

For most of us, development from earliest childhood to retirement and death is a struggle to meld these contradictory drives of altruism and selfishness into a functioning human personality that produces more benefit than damage, not only for ourselves, but for others. One could describe this as a struggle between the saint and the sinner, between the superego and the id, or between morality and the drive for material survival and prosperity. Professionals are clearly not exempt from this human condition. Many professional roles intensify the problem because they carry both the expectation for public service and the opportunity for financial aggrandizement.

Doubts about whether it is appropriate to describe this as a dilemma could also be raised on definitional grounds. I have posed the choice as one between service to the client and success as a professional.[15] One might argue that the successful professional is one who serves the client's interests, and therefore there is no opposition in the two goals. Success, as I use it, is a cultural judgment or concept. In the wider society and in professional circles as well, success is often defined largely, if not exclusively, in terms of attaining material success or prestigious positions, or by competitive success in the pecking order of the profession. The index to such success is very often income. The correlation between the three indices to success is high, but not always perfect. Judges and professors enjoy high prestige and lower incomes, while divorce or criminal lawyers may enjoy larger incomes and lower prestige. Desire to attain high incomes, positions of great power, or social esteem can push any professional to make choices that are difficult to defend morally.

Although all professionals are to a greater or lesser degree under pressure to attain culturally defined goals of success, most feel that propriety requires them to disguise or hide such aspirations. This is what makes the problem of this book a subject that, if not taboo, is at least avoided in most ethical discussions.[16] Norman Podhoretz, a writer known for articulating conventional and conservative positions, has described the clandestine nature of the dilemma in a slightly different context:

> On the one hand, our culture teaches us to shape our lives in accordance with the hunger for worldly things; on the other hand, it spitefully contrives to make us ashamed of the presence of those hungers in ourselves and to deprive us as far as possible of any pleasure in their satisfaction.[17]

For the client, this context presents a problem, not a dilemma. Many services are so specialized or so technical that consumers cannot make an informed judgment about when they need services, who should provide those services, or the scope, nature, and extent of the services they need. Obtaining reliable information on which to base sensible decisions about purchases is an endemic problem to any market system of service delivery. The natural tendency for any prospective client is to consult a specialist, normally someone in the business of providing such services. Encouraging customers to ask for advice and to rely on the provider's answers creates a special relationship of trust, one actively encouraged by most professions and many businesses. In such a "supportive" environment, the client may be inclined to let his guard down and relax the normal suspicions he would bring to a transaction with a provider he perceives as a purely self-seeking business person. If the advice is that the services are needed, it is natural to ask that same expert you have been encouraged to trust to do the job.

When an unnecessary service is "sold" to a client, there is a substantial cost. A part of the client's assets that would have been available for other purposes is needlessly expended. If this pattern is common, we have a social problem as well, because a significant percentage of gross national income or of consumers' disposable dollars is diverted to provide unnecessary, if not undeserved, income to a particular professional group and away from other potentially desirable expenditures.[18]

Since the dilemma is faced by any supplier of nonroutine services, this analysis could apply to all providers asked for advice. The discussion will be restricted to those occupations that are considered to be professions. Professionals are distinguished from other providers not merely by their level of technical knowledge, competence, and specialized training, but also by a commitment to a set of ethics and an obligation to serve clients faithfully. This duty of service is, in many professions, formally assumed in the oath administered to new members when they are admitted as licensed professionals. While one could argue that the same ethical obligations should apply to all occupations, the codes make it explicit, or clearly implicit, in the professions and thus heighten the dilemma for individual practitioners. Many of my examples will be from the venerable professions of law and medicine, but not because I think the problems of abuse are more acute there. These professions are best for analysis because they have clear ethical codes, a tradition of professional education that includes some ethical training, and a long history of trying, without conspicuous success, to control unethical conduct by the amoral or immoral members of their professions.

ARE ALL PROFESSIONALS FACED WITH THE SAME DILEMMA?

To show the clearest case, my analysis assumes an autonomous self-employed professional who contracts directly with a client. The dilemma is simplest and starkest there. However, this model does not describe the majority of members in professions like law, medicine, stockbrokering, or accounting, and very few members indeed of professions like social work, nursing, or teaching. If not self-employed, the professional has a duty to both her employer and her client. To the extent that the employer is pressured to succeed, the demands placed by superiors on the employed professional intensify her problems. She has lost autonomous control over the context of the dilemma, and her choices may become even more skewed toward the success horn of the dilemma.

Many professions, such as nursing, journalism, engineering, and accounting, face ethical choices similar to the dilemma I am describing, but their difficulty is not the temptation to provide unnecessary or excessive services to pad income. Some, such as nurses, accountants, or engineers, are ordinarily supporting or subordinate professionals. They are required to support or assist supervising professionals, such as doctors, managers, or architects. These supervisors are usually the ones choosing to provide services, necessary or otherwise. In the course of their duties, subordinate professionals may be asked to perform services they know are excessive or even to falsify records to disguise the unethical activity of superiors. Their dilemma, then, is between being a whistle-blower to protect the ethical professional obligations they owe to the client or the public, and passively assisting or watching the exploitation of the client. Does loyalty to the team and the employer override the obligation of service to the client and to the public? If they do not cooperate with unethical superiors, they may lose their job or lose that particular client. This economic pressure, whether overt or anticipated, can tilt the weighing of the success horn over the service horn of the dilemma by subordinate professionals. They acquiesce in the unethical conduct of supervisors.

A major role of certain other professionals, such as journalists and public accountants acting as auditors, is to provide information the public is asked to trust. Financial pressure from advertisers or clients may be used to persuade them to lie or slant information. As in the dominant dilemma, the more difficult and pervasive choices are not in outright lying (analogous to providing totally unnecessary services), but rather the slanting or shading of the truth (analogous to extending or padding necessary services). The latter is harder to detect and easier to justify.

Because I think the ethical dilemma is ultimately the same for these groups as for the independent or autonomous professional, there will often be reference to or discussion of their problems. My primary focus, however, began with and remains the dilemma arising out of the role conflict when the advisor on the necessity for services and the provider of those services is an autonomous, self-employed professional.

CHOICE AND INTERNAL OR EXTERNAL MOTIVATORS

To describe the situation facing a professional as a dilemma implies a problem of choice. For this description to be accurate, it requires a perception on the part of the professional that she can act in one of two or more ways and an ability to do either action. If the situation takes on the full character of a dilemma, there must be motives, drives, or causes impelling the actor in each direction. Each element poses its own difficulties. Does the professional actually perceive that there are actually two possibilities for action? If so, does she feel that she is free to do one or the other? Is she pushed in one direction or the other? What are the types, strengths, and rewards of these competing motivations?

Whether the individual professional is aware of the dilemma or is capable of recognizing it, this situation can clearly be described as a dilemma that must concern society. Many professionals appear to be choosing improper or unacceptable courses of action, at least some of the time. What are the ways in which these choices are made by individual professionals? How does the society or any individual affect or change these professional choices?

Here we need to make a distinction. On the one hand, we can think about the motivations of the professional who is making a choice as internal to the actor. Then we are likely to be talking about values or conscience, those things that push the actor from the inside.[19] On the other hand, we could describe the motivations influencing the professional as external. Here the analysis would be about financial rewards or penalties, esteem or disrespect from society or peers, the granting or withholding of power—all those factors that seem to pull the individual.

It has become fashionable in this century to think of human motivation as external. The human being is reduced to the status of a responder to external stimuli. This way of describing human motivation may be dictated by a desire to change or influence individual actions. Only with time and difficulty can we through education, modelling, or psychological therapy have a significant impact on the internal motivations of individuals. Yet, if we use the term *ethics*, it is this internal realm we are describing. If ethical choices being made by professionals are undesirable, others' reactions in the community may be reduced to clucking disapprovingly, the only reaction appropriate to those actions in the area of autonomy or choice when we disapprove. Such a mild and ineffective reaction to unacceptable behavior is unsatisfactory. We then feel compelled to restrain the choice by use of external motivators of varying degrees of strength and compulsion, thus removing it from the area of freedom or autonomy.

If a central element of the concept of a professional is the autonomy and expertise each individual possesses, we should be more comfortable in concentrating on internal motivations rather than on external motivations that, if effective, would impose much greater constraints on individual autonomy.

It is possible to describe the primary dilemma as a struggle between the ethical realm of internal motivations and the realm of pressure from the outside to act contrary to the professional's internal values. It might be more accurate to say that the dilemma is totally internal to the acting professional, that is, that both the pressure to be ethical and the pressure to be successful have been internalized. A third possibility is to regard the professional as one who is merely a responder to external pressures pushing both toward decency and toward success. If we believe the last possibility is the best description, we start by lining up and counting the pressures that push her in the two different directions. If we do not like the current product of the way these pressures multiply, we could try to increase the number and strength of those pressures that push in the direction we want.

We cannot effectively choose strategies to alter the ethical choices being made by professionals without some decision, however tentative it might be, about whether the motivating pressures are internal or external.

NOTES

1. See Gina Kolata, "Rate of Hysterectomies Puzzles Experts," *New York Times*, Sept. 20, 1988, C1; James Barron, "Unnecessary Surgery," *New York Times*, April 16, 1989, Section 6, Part 2, 25.

2. Such claims may underrepresent the problem, as unethical choices are often hidden and hard to discover.

3. The decision by either a plaintiff's lawyer to bring an action or a defendant's lawyer to resist a claim carries with it not only the cost of the advising lawyer's charges, but the fees that must be paid to the other side. Since many judgments as well as litigation costs are often paid by liability insurance, these additional costs are passed on to the general public through increased insurance premiums.

4. Both the insurance agent and the stockbroker are paid by commission and thus are compensated only if the transaction goes through.

5. This dilemma extends far beyond the recognized professions to include such occupations as automobile mechanics, electricians, and plumbers, although the choice may be less personally wrenching in those occupations, where there are no formal ethical codes that mandate protecting the welfare of customers.

6. See later discussion on internal commitment in Chapter 2.

7. See *The Oxford English Dictionary*, vol. 2 (Oxford: Clarendon Press, 1933, 1969), 362; *The Random House Dictionary of the English Language*, unabridged ed. (New York: Random House, 1973), 403.

8. John Kultgen, *Ethics and Professionalism* (Philadelphia: University of Pennsylvania Press, 1988), 256.

9. *Pro bono publico* is the technical term describing work by a lawyer undertaken as a public service for which she receives no compensation. Performance of *pro bono* work is often considered a professional duty. Of course, lawyers may evade this responsibility or perform it in a perfunctory manner. There is no question that the *pro bono* activities of Abe Fortas were undertaken voluntarily and performed with all the vast intelligence and skill for which he could otherwise charge enormous fees.

10. Bruce Allen Murphy, *Fortas: The Rise and Ruin of a Supreme Court Justice* (New York: William Morrow & Co., 1988), 82–85.

11. Ibid, 86.

12. 372 U.S. 335 (1963).

13. The best discussion of this case and the role of Abe Fortas is found in Anthony Lewis, *Gideon's Trumpet* (New York: Random House, 1964).

14. See Murphy, *Fortas*, Chapter 14.

15. This might more accurately be described as a choice involving a number of persons or entities. One must choose among service to the client, to oneself, to colleagues, to the public, and to the profession. See the discussion on role conflicts in Chapter 3.

16. See Norman Podhoretz, *Making It* (New York: Random House, 1967) for a discussion about an analogous dilemma and a similar reaction among members of New York City's literary circles. His thesis is that artists who are supposed to be concerned only with artistic goals are obsessed by making money and attaining social success. The book was savaged by critics who thought his book might be descriptively wrong and was certainly simplistically obvious. See Frederick Raphael, "What Makes Norman Run," *New York Times Book Review*, Jan. 7, 1968, 4:

> What makes Norman run and, more important, what Norman now suddenly perceives makes most of them run, are those two very American urges, the wish to be somebody and to make a buck. No surprises there, surely? But Podhoretz is dealing with a section of the community and a particular specimen—himself— which has systematically repressed these common desires.

The intensity of critical reactions might be some evidence that Podhoretz was right.

17. Podhoretz, *Making It*, xiii.

18. Obviously the money coming to the professional, whether deserved or not, will be spent, so there is no diminution in total spending. The question is who will spend it. This is, however, an important distinction, not only economically but as a matter of public policy or social goals. There are a variety of needs in society. Any maldistribution or distortion in allocating resources to meeting the whole range of public needs may prevent worthwhile ends from being attained.

19. This terminology is not intended to take the position that values or conscience are innate or fixed, but only that they are fixed substantially prior to the time of choice.

2

The Professional

To understand the professionals' dilemma, we need to know not only what the dilemma is, but also what *professionals* are, or at least, for purposes of this study, who count as professionals. Obviously, they are members of a profession, and that points to the first area of inquiry. What does being a member of a profession entail?

EXTERNAL INSIGNIA OF PROFESSIONALISM

Profession is a more limited grouping than *occupation* or *employment*. It is a linguistic concept and for its meaning and content we might look to some general definition such as the one in the *Oxford English Dictionary*:

III. 6. The occupation which one professes to be skilled in and to follow. a. A vocation in which a professed knowledge of some department of learning or science is used in its application to the affairs of others or in the practice of an art founded upon it. Applied *spec.* to the three learned professions of divinity, law, and medicine; also to the military profession.[1]

Like all definitions, this is of limited use in identifying which occupations belong inside the concept and which should be excluded. Borderline cases here, as everywhere, are difficult.

Other approaches are possible. One is by defining characteristics; that is, listing certain essential characteristics such as the existence of a professional organization, state licensing, professional schools, professional journals, codes of ethics, and relatively high social status for members, and then identifying as professions those occupations that possess these external characteristics.

A second method is to look at the central or paradigm case. One looks at those occupational groups that are generally recognized in contemporary society as professions. We could identify each profession sociologically by the territory of human expertise or specialization it controls or monopolizes.[2] Although this territory could then be the identifying insignia of a particular profession, this procedure is of limited utility in helping decide which occupations should be designated as professions.

Finally, we could regard *profession* as a functional concept. Professionals have specified expertise that no one else adequately has. They sell that to clients who rely on them. Therefore, persons who do not have the expected expertise and are not trustworthy[3] should not be entitled to "professional" status.[4]

Whichever approach we take, some occupational groups, like doctors and lawyers, will always be included. Others will always be excluded, such as sales clerks, plumbers, and auto mechanics. There is fluidity as occupational groups strive to achieve the social and economic status of professionals. The aspiring occupations tend to follow a pattern that often begins by adopting a different name and then creates the exterior symbols of professionalism by establishing professional schools, lobbying for state licensing, and promulgating a code of ethics.[5] Despite adopting the trappings, some groups fail to achieve social recognition as a profession. Others succeed. Today nurses, accountants, journalists, and engineers are generally recognized as professionals, whereas a hundred years ago they would not have been. If by *professional* we mean a commitment to high-level expert service provided in a trustworthy relationship devoted to protecting the welfare of the client, then we should encourage more occupations to make such a commitment and as a consequence receive recognition for being professional.

There will always be borderline occupations. An interesting example is corporate or business managers, who enjoy high social status, but do not possess many identifying features, such as an identifiable body of expertise, a code of ethics, or a clear professional organization.[6] Corporate managers tend to be employers of or users of professionals. They fall much more into the category of clients. They are, however, usually knowledgeable, sophisticated, and often demanding clients.

I am not concerned with developing a list of "in" and "out" occupations, but rather with analyzing a dilemma facing all professionals. Before being clearly faced with that dilemma, individual practitioners must be a part of certain social structures and relationships. They must be believed to possess a body of expertise and be consulted by other people, they must be licensed, they should have attended a professional school, and they must be obligated to follow a code of ethics which, if not formally articulated, is at least generally recognized as binding on members of the occupational group. Thus, I am defining as professionals those people who face the dilemma, rather than identifying persons as professionals and then asking whether they face the dilemma or not.

Since throughout the book I will be using the elements of expertise, professional education, professional organization, state licensing, and a code of ethics in analyzing the dilemma and its associated problems, any group not possessing these characteristics does not qualify as a profession for the purpose of this study.

A professional has been defined as one "engaged in one of the learned or skilled professions, or in a calling considered socially superior to a trade or handicraft."[7] Many occupations clearly excluded from the professions, such as electricians, auto mechanics, and plumbers, possess a high level of expertise not possessed by general members of the public. Some of these occupations, such as electricians, are required to be licensed. They often tend to have occupational organizations, but these are usually labelled "unions." What is it that distinguishes these "trade" occupations from the professions?

It has been argued that the type of expertise or knowledge could be the distinguishing factor. "Certainly all [theorists about professions] agreed that a profession was an occupational group with some abstract skill, one that required extensive training. It was not applied in a purely routine fashion, but required revised application case by case."[8] This distinction between abstract knowledge requiring case by case application as contrasted with routine knowledge and procedures may not be defensible as a distinguishing characteristic between profession and occupation. Is the knowledge of a good auto mechanic less abstract or less dependent on diagnostic skills that that of an engineer or an accountant? The professional must possess some level of expertise that is not easily acquired or that, if practiced on other people when the provider is not properly expert, could cause damage. When this expertise is not general knowledge, the customer has difficulty in judging whether a provider has expertise, as well as the extent of her competence. This is a critical factor promoting the conflict of interest discussed in this book.

The claim of a profession to a monopoly is justified only on grounds of protecting the public from dangerous charlatans or well-meaning incompetents. The demand for autonomy that is closely related to the claim of exclusivity can of course serve just as well as a defense or mask against accountability of those members of the profession who do not have the required expertise or indeed for the entire profession not possessing the sort of expertise that justifies exclusivity and autonomy. Boundary disputes between professional groups such as lawyers and accountants or doctors and nurses often turn on whether such expertise exists and which groups are entitled to claim it.

I feel more comfortable focusing on the relationship with the customer as the distinguishing characteristic, a position that makes sense in terms of the thesis of this book. Mere occupations do not claim a special commitment to the welfare of their customers. The professional asks for a relationship of trust. The concomitant ethical obligation is what really distinguishes the professional from other occupations. In my analysis, these twin requirements of possessing a special expertise not easily understood by lay people and of being ethical and trustworthy in relationships with clients and the public are what distinguish professions from other occupations.

THE INTERNAL COMMITMENT

The external marks of the professional described in the previous section, such as possession of expertise, membership in a professional organization, being licensed, giving formal allegiance to an ethical code, and having a recognized social status, all represent a dimension where the individual has only limited choice. One can aspire to professional status, but achieving it depends on acceptance and admittance by others. This social acceptance proceeds through a series of steps: (1) being admitted to a professional school, (2) passing the courses, which signifies that adequate competence in various types and levels of technical expertise has been attained, (3) passing the state certification examination, (4) being licensed,[9] and finally (5) locating or establishing a position of employment or service within the profession.

To qualify as a professional, particularly for my purposes, another factor is more critical. There is an internal dimension, which is acquiring the *character* of a professional. This is a matter of individual choice and commitment. The professional character has at least two components. The first is to master and practice the expertise of the profession to the highest level of competence the individual can manage. The external standards require minimum or adequate competence. The internal standards of a professional aspire to the highest possible level of competence.

The second component is a commitment to use these high levels of competence to serve others. In the first instance, the duty of service runs to the client, but it can run to fellow professionals, to others who stand in some relationship to the client such as family members or business associates, or even to bystanders, and on occasion to the community as a whole. One of the ethical dilemmas facing a professional occurs when the interests of a particular client clash with the broader interests of the public, or some part of it. This commitment not only to the client but also to public service is part of the tradition of all professions. Each member of a profession is faced with a choice. She can make this internal commitment of service, or she can masquerade as a professional.

The dilemma discussed here will be a real and enduring problem only for those who make this internal commitment.

Of course, professionalism is not an all-or-nothing category. It is a matter of degree. Those who are competent, but not at the highest levels, and those who are ethical in aspirations and instincts, but do not always act so, can be considered professional. It is only those not striving for competence or ethical conduct who are unworthy of being so considered.

The preceding discussion suggests that making this internal commitment or deciding to masquerade as a professional while pursuing material ambitions is a matter of individual choice. It has been argued, however, that the professions have begun to constitute a new "class" in society distinct from Marxist or sociological classes. "The class consciousness of professionals appears in the ideology of professionalism itself, in the common speech that Gouldner has called the 'culture of critical discourse,' and in the widespread political beliefs of the new class."[10] If professionalism is the ideology of the professional class and that professionalism contains a commitment to professional ethics, then one cannot become a member of the class without adopting this ideology. Accepting the ideology of the class to which one belongs is only to a limited extent a matter of individual choice.

This contrast between external marks of professionalism and the internal commitment to a professional character reflects a difference not only in how professions are defined, but also in how they are legitimated. In the nineteenth century, the character of those belonging to professional groups was an important part of the demonstration to the public at large that the group's members should be regarded as professionals. This was caught in the eighteenth- and nineteenth-century concept of gentlemanliness and the character traits that that concept represented. The clergy, lawyers, doctors, and military officers usually aspired to and represented these traits. In the twentieth century, efficiency, knowledge, and techniques have tended to become the legitimating factors. If the professional possesses the abstract knowledge, has mastered the techniques of the profession, and uses these efficiently, should her personal character be at all relevant? The thesis of this book is that those techniques are not likely to be mastered or used effectively without the character traits that come from the commitment to service to client and the public.[11]

THE AUTONOMY OF A PROFESSIONAL

Professionals make a claim to a high degree of autonomy or discretion in the way they practice their profession vis-à-vis clients. This is related to the demand of the profession for exclusive jurisdiction and under this group demand each member claims a concomitant share of that exclusive jurisdiction.

A jurisdictional claim made before the public is generally a claim for the legitimate control of a particular kind of work. This control means first and foremost a right to perform the work as professionals see fit. Along with the right to perform the work as it wishes, a profession normally also claims rights to exclude other workers as deemed necessary, to dominate public definitions of the tasks concerned, and indeed to impose professional definitions of the tasks on competing professions. Public jurisdiction, in short, is a claim of both social and cultural authority.[12]

Stated differently, this is a claim to be free of governmental regulation in the way the profession is practiced and in the judgments made by the practitioner. It can also be a claim to be free of regulation by the professional group as well.

Alasdair MacIntyre has observed that, in contemporary western industrial countries,

there are only two alternative modes of social life open to us, one in which the free and arbitrary choices of individuals are sovereign and one in which the bureaucracy is sovereign, precisely so that it may limit the free arbitrary choices of individuals. Given this deep cultural agreement, it is unsurprising that the politics of modern societies oscillate between a freedom which is nothing but a lack of regulation of individual behavior and forms of collectivist control designed only to limit the anarchy of self-interest. . . . [B]oth ways of life are in the long run intolerable.[13]

There is a tension between these two polar positions for the professional as well. Our ideal picture of a professional is a self-employed, autonomous practitioner. The reality is very different for many. The professional group and the state and its licensing authorities are bureaucracies claiming the right to limit the autonomy of the professional. More importantly, a substantial majority of all professionals are employed inside bureaucratic organizations. If the professional's expertise requires a high level of autonomy, there is an inconsistency in having a person who does not possess the expertise telling an expert how to do her job. At the same time, inside all bureaucratic or complex organizations there is a need to coordinate and integrate the expertise of many different specialties. This is the role of the manager.

The danger to the autonomy of professionals is not merely from overt government or professional regulation. To return to MacIntyre's analysis:

> Contemporary moral experience as a consequence has a paradoxical character. For each of us is taught to see himself or herself as an autonomous moral agent; but each of us also becomes engaged by modes of practice, aesthetic or bureaucratic, which involve us in manipulative relationships with others. Seeking to protect the autonomy we have learned to prize, we aspire ourselves not to be manipulated by others; seeking to incarnate our own principles and standpoint in the world of practice, we find no way open to us to do so except by directing towards others those very manipulative modes of relationships which each of us aspires to resist in our own case.[14]

A professional's relationships with clients, other professionals, and bureaucratic superiors are often manipulative, and this runs both ways. The professional may use her expertise and power to control clients. Clients who are desirable customers may use their option to hire from among competing professionals as a means to pressure the practitioner. This problem of client and professional autonomy in a manipulative environment will reappear in Chapter 9 in the discussion about the importance of mutually satisfying agreements.

There are close analogies between the central dilemma and the tension caused by demanding the autonomy to do what the professional thinks best and, at the same time, being subject to the control exercised by bureaucratic organizations of which the professional is a member.

Being embedded in social bureaucracies is not the only constraint on professional autonomy. Another increasingly important limitation is technology. By this, I mean something broader than just machines and the procedures by which they are used. It is essentially what Jacques Ellul calls *technique*, which he defines as follows: "The term *technique*, as I use it, does not mean machines, technology, or this or that procedure for attaining an end. In our technological society, *technique is the totality of methods rationally arrived at and having absolute efficiency* (for a given stage of development) in *every* field of human activity."[15]

Professions differ markedly on the extent to which they use and are used by their technology. The most obviously constrained is the medical profession, which has been transformed by the technologies of diagnostic machinery, the availability of chemical therapies, and the revolution in surgical instruments and technologies. Once a technology is available, the doctor has no choice but to use it and to follow the course of professional treatment dictated by the technology. As Jacques Ellul has expressed this:

A surgical operation which was formerly not feasible but can now be performed is not an object of choice. It simply is. Here we see the prime aspect of technical automatism. Technique itself, *ipso facto* and without indulgence or possible discussion, selects among the means to be employed. The human being is no longer in any sense the agent of choice. Let no one say that man is the agent of technical progress . . . and that it is he who chooses among possible techniques. In reality, he neither is nor does anything of the sort. He is a device for recording effects and results obtained by various techniques. He does not make a choice of complex and, in some ways, human motives. He can decide only in favor of the technique that gives the maximum efficiency. But this is not choice. A machine could effect the same operation.[16]

Neither the development nor the use of technology can be turned off or ignored. In addition to the automatic dynamic of technical progress described by Ellul, ethical obligations and the fear of legal liability constrain the professional against discretionary choices that do not make full use of available technology.

Other professional groups that may have become prisoners of their technology are engineers and architects. Even those professions normally thought to be free of technological constraints, such as lawyers or journalists, are increasingly controlled by communications technology, such as word processors, electronic communication, and computer-stored libraries. The computer is a technology no professional is free to disregard.

CONCLUDING QUESTION: WHO DETERMINES PROFESSIONALISM?

Who decides whether an occupation should be regarded as a profession? Is it for the members of an occupational group to choose and by adopting the various insignia of a profession thus become one? Then social recognition along with state licensing and approval would merely be acknowledgements of that choice. Is it rather for the broader community, whether we regard it as the state, the culture, or public opinion, to decide that the relationship between practitioner and client calls for a different set of expectations—fidelity, trust, concern, and fiduciary notions? Because the members of an occupation who aspire to become professionals are seeking social status and recognition, along with the other advantages such as higher income and greater autonomy, the reaction of society is critical and social recognition is not automatic. There are always fewer recognized professions than there are aspirants for that status. The process of becoming a profession is not exclusively controlled by the occupation or by the society. Only those professions whose members aspire to becoming professionals have a chance. However, it is not the aspiration but the recognition that is determinative, and that recognition is controlled by the broader society or the public.

The hypothesis I would like to suggest is that, whether such social recognition is given, so that the occupation comes to be considered a profession, turns not solely but very importantly on the nature of the relationship between the occupation and the customer and the ethical requirements such a relationship imposes. Those ethical requirements will be developed in the next chapter.

NOTES

1. *The Oxford English Dictionary*, vol. 8 (Oxford: Clarendon Press, 1933, 1969), 1427.

2. For such an approach, see Andrew Abbott, *The System of Professions: An essay on the Division of Expert Labor* (Chicago: University of Chicago Press, 1988).

3. The client may not be concerned with whether the professional is trustworthy or moral in other arenas and, to the extent that the client is looking solely for the expertise, he may not be concerned with the trustworthiness of the professional as long as he receives the needed services, except that the client will not tolerate the professional's dishonesty in dealing with him. Here, of course, we are concerned not with whether such an expert is acceptable to the client, but whether he is entitled to the status of professional.

4. For a discussion of functional concepts like this, see Alasdair MacIntyre, *After Virtue* (Notre Dame, Ind.: University of Notre Dame Press, 1981), 54–55.

5. One ordering of events in the march toward professionalism is listed in Abbott, *The System of Professions*, 16. He lists the sequence as:

1. First (national) professional association
2. First governmentally sponsored licensing legislation
3. First professional examinations
4. First professional school separate from some other profession
5. First university-based professional education
6. First ethics code
7. First national-level journal
8. First accreditation of schools (U.S.) or certification by association (England)

He then proceeds to evaluate exactly how the historical evolution of various professions follows this sequence. He finds it is followed closely in some and not at all in others.

6. Many corporate executives are members of recognized professions, such as law, accounting, or engineering, but do not, when they become managers, rely primarily on that professional background, nor would they accept accountability to those professions for decisions they make in their capacity as corporate executives. Andrew Abbott argues that business managers do not constitute a profession because they lack any particular abstract knowledge as their province. See Abbott, *The System of Professions*, 103: "The real problem with business management [as a profession] is the tenuous connection between the various abstractions applied to the area and the actual work of managers."

7. *Oxford English Dictionary*, 1428.

8. "[A]bstract knowledge is the foundation of an effective definition of professions. Many occupations fight for turf, but only professions expand their cognitive dominion by using abstract knowledge to annex new areas, to define them as their own proper work. My theory of professional development thus creates my definition of professions. As is traditional, abstract knowledge is central. But the justification for it is new; knowledge is the currency of competition." Abbott, *The System of Professions*, 102.

9. It might appear that passing the state certification examination is the same as being licensed, but there are additional requirements for licensing, such as residency and requisite moral character.

10. Abbott, *The System of Professions*, 174.

11. This paragraph is based on the discussion in Abbott, *The System of Professions*, 190–92.

12. Ibid, 60.

13. MacIntyre, *After Virtue*, 33.

14. Ibid, 66.

15. Jacques Ellul, *The Technological Society* (New York: Vintage Books, 1964), xxv.

16. Ibid, 80.

3

The Ethical Expectation

If we define ethics as normative guidelines specifying what a professional ought to do in order to do the right or the proper thing,[1] this dilemma does not seem to raise substantial ethical difficulties. There should be no serious doubt about the ethical duty of doctors, lawyers, stockbrokers, or any other professionals. They ought to refrain from furnishing unnecessary, dishonest, or inappropriate services. Any difficulties would be only along the edges of the obligation as to exactly what kinds of activities it covers or in problems of application. This chapter is intended to ground the ethical obligation, to explain its extensions, and to show how it has been articulated in various ethical codes and practices of the different professions.

Hardly anybody would dispute the proposition that it is unethical for a professional to sell unnecessary or unwanted services to a client. A few might rely on the proposition that a professional merely sells services in the market and it is not unethical for a participant in a market economy to sell unnecessary services that are accepted by the other party, unless the professional engages in narrowly defined acts of fraud or duress.[2]

The professional's obligation not to provide unnecessary services is made quite explicit in many codes of professional ethics, and is clear at least by implication in all the others. Why then spend any time grounding, justifying, or explaining this ethical imperative? First, it is often violated, which indicates that the spirit of the obligation, as distinguished from its letter, may not always be understood or accepted. Another reason is to determine the strength of the obligation. Is it a powerful and primary duty, or merely subsidiary and not of great importance? Finally, if we decide that the degree of deviation from the standard is greater than can be tolerated, a clear understanding of the purposes for the ethical prescription will help in selecting strategies to enhance compliance.

What type of justification is possible? Alasdair MacIntyre has suggested that ethical thought in modern history has evolved through three stages:

> The scheme of moral decline which these remarks presuppose would, as I suggested earlier, be one which required the discrimination of three distinct stages; a first at which evaluation and more especially moral theory and practice embody genuine objective and impersonal standards which provide rational justification; a second stage at which there are unsuccessful attempts to maintain the objectivity and impersonality of moral judgments, but during which the project of providing rational justifications both by means of and for the standards continuously breaks down; and a third stage at which theories of an emotivist kind secure wide implicit acceptance because of a general implicit recognition in practice, though not in explicit theory, that claims to objectivity and impersonality cannot be made good.[3]

MacIntyre is correct in saying that the ethical standards have broken down. They can be reconstituted in terms that are objective and not merely emotivist. My discussion will have utilitarian elements because I will be concerned with the consequences of choices that might be made. There can be a functional justification arising from the role of the professional. It is possible to ground this obligation of service to the client and others in reasoning that all rational people should accept. This rationale would be based on the requirement of truth telling and of not disappointing trust once it has been asked for and given. Whichever of these different sets of justifications is acceptable to the reader is not critical for my analysis, so long as the ethical injunction is accepted by professionals as one carrying substantial weight. Only then does the situation become a genuine dilemma for professionals who are being subjected to social and financial pressures toward success.

ROLE CONFLICTS

The sociological concept of *role* defines different relationships that exist between the professional and others. The others may be individual persons, groups, or larger entities. Those that are important for this discussion include:

1. The professional and client
2. The professional, if not self-employed, and employer
3. The professional and fellow professionals
4. The professional and members of related, competing, or subordinate professions
5. The professional and the profession (as an entity or group)
6. The professional and society

One can identify the responsibilities or duties owed by the professional to each of the others in the various roles. These responsibilities often conflict, and the professional cannot equally satisfy the duties owed to the various others when roles conflict. One of the major responsibilities of formal or informal ethical codes is to give guidelines for resolving those conflicts by indicating weights or priorities belonging to role responsibilities.

The primary focus here is on the first role relationship, that of the professional and the client. The conflict causing the dilemma described in Chapter 1 might be viewed as subroles in the professional-client relationship, that of counsellor and that of provider. It is important to recognize that the professional has responsibilities or duties to herself as well as to the client. Thus, conflicts emerge from this basic relationship. Some conflicts arising from other roles will be present, although muted, in this analysis, particularly those between the professional and employer, and the professional and colleagues.

An interesting example of a dilemma arising from two ethical duties in conflict other than as in our primary dilemma where an ethical duty and a prudential interest conflict is one facing lawyers and probably other professionals as well. There are strong informal ethical rules about how one treats fellow professionals, such as in matters of courtesy, accommodation, and refraining from criticism. Often the duties owed a client conflict with these informal duties owed fellow professionals. Many lawyers will sacrifice the interests of clients to satisfy the duties owed fellow professionals and will justify this with the argument that they must do business with these other lawyers for the rest of their career, so future clients would suffer if they do not enjoy the confidence and accommodations other professionals can offer.[4]

An interesting query is whether in those professions defining themselves as occupying a counselling or advising role, such as social worker or psychologist, the dilemma becomes more muted or perhaps disappears. These professionals are often employees in large organizations, so the pressure on them, rather than aspirations toward financial aggrandizement, would often be to carry out the employer's agenda and thereby secure advancement within the organization. That does not change the dilemma, but merely the source of pressure along the horn of success.

THE ETHICAL INJUNCTION:
TO PROMOTE THE CLIENT'S INTEREST BY
NOT PROVIDING UNNECESSARY SERVICES

I am positing the professional in two conflicting roles or subroles. There is no conflict at the ethical level. If professionals are approached in their role as counsellor to advise clients about whether a certain service is necessary, their duty arises out of the nature of the relationship. When one invites or creates an atmosphere of trust and then is asked for advice, the duty is to respond honestly. The liability that is raised by an intentionally deceptive answer is not only ethical; there could be legal liability as well for deceit or breach of contract.[5]

In the role of provider of services, there is equally an obligation not to perform unnecessary services. This does not arise so much from the relationship of trust, as it does from the concept of being a professional. Professionals hold themselves out as people who possess special competence and expertise. Competent performance certainly encompasses knowing which services the client really needs as well as performing only those services.

Not only is there the element of trust in the professional relationship, but an imbalance of power, arising from the professional's monopoly of information and expertise. This makes it inappropriate to analyze the relationship between a professional and a client in purely economic or market terms. It is much more a fiduciary relationship where neither the ethical nor legal obligations developed for true market transactions apply. Here, we are concerned with not legal but ethical obligations. Is it ethically appropriate to say to professionals that they owe clients the same duties of fidelity, concern, and care expected of trustees who legally own property that they must administer for the welfare of a beneficiary or required of a guardian who has the responsibility for an incompetent ward? Of course, the typical client is not incompetent and wants to retain control over his affairs, but he needs honest and reliable assistance from the professional. It might be too strong to define this as a fiduciary relationship, but it could be called quasi-fiduciary to indicate its middle position between a market relationship and a fiduciary one.

When one professional performs both roles of counselling and providing services for a client, it is the role of provider that produces the problem. The counselling role is merely to give advice and, as the compensation would normally be the same whatever the advice, there is no conflict arising from self-interest. The provider of the services, however, is compensated for the difficulty of the problem and for the time expended on the services, so the provision of unnecessary or excessive services produces more income. The role of provider creates the conflict between self-interest and disinterested decision making.

RULES AND ETHICS

An important distinction between rules and ethics was made by Alasdair MacIntyre:

It is yet another of Nietzche's merits that he joins to his critique of Enlightenment moralities a sense of their failure to address adequately, let alone to answer the question: what sort of person am I to become? This is in a way an inescapable question in that an answer to it is given *in practice* in each human life. But for characteristically modern moralities it is a question to be approached only by indirection. The primary question from their standpoint has concerned rules: what rules ought we to follow? And why ought we to obey them? . . . Rules become the primary concept of the moral life. Qualities of character then generally come to be prized only because they will lead us to follow the right set of rules.[6]

If we are concerned with the ethics of professionals, we should focus on the character of a professional and the kinds of traits and dispositions that demands. Mere compliance with certain specific rules of ethical codes is not enough. This distinction will take on greater significance when we discuss education in professional ethics in Chapter 12.

If ethics are viewed as sets of rules and principles, the ethical obligation at the heart of this study, which requires the professional to prefer the client's interest over self-interest, is intended to be a principle, rather than a rule. Here, I draw on a distinction made by Ronald Dworkin between rules on the one hand and principles[7] on the other. According to Dworkin:

The difference between . . . principles and . . . rules is a logical distinction. Both sets of standards point to particular decisions about . . . [8] obligation in particular circumstances, but they differ in the character of the direction they give. Rules are applicable in an all-or-nothing fashion. If the facts a rule stipulates are given, then either the rule is valid, in which case the answer it supplies must be accepted, or it is not, in which case it contributes nothing to the decision.[9]

A principle . . . does not even purport to set out conditions that make its application necessary. Rather, it states a reason that argues in one direction, but does not necessitate a particular decision. . . . Principles have a dimension that rules do not—the dimension of weight or importance.[10]

Dworkin's concept of "principle" is illuminating. First, it emphasizes that the ethical injunction is founded on morality, rather than on reasons of social or political policy. Second, it stresses that the obligation does not automatically control decision, but rather has weight or strength in the context of balancing this injunction against other principles, policies, or goals. Thus, it more realistically catches the competing pressures on professionals and the process of balancing their decision requires.

Why is it important to emphasize this as an ethical, rather than a legal, duty? When codes are viewed legalistically, there is a tendency to think that compliance with the rules, rather than with the spirit of the code, is all that is required. There are a number of contexts in which professionals are called upon to exercise judgment and where a professional's self-serving decision could be defended in terms of literal compliance with the ethical codes or with the strict requirements of the law, but such a decision would violate the spirit of the ethical injunction to protect the client's interests.[11]

If, instead of approaching ethics as a system of discrete but related rules defining the professional's ethical responsibilities, we wanted to identify the virtues attached to this status or role, what would they be? These virtues would identify the internal professional character that is the bedrock of the ethical practitioner.

One virtue would be *competence* in the expertise of the profession which, in a technical and specialized world, is clearly a major virtue (as well as a commodity that can be sold).[12] What is at stake here is not the obligation to achieve minimum competence, but to strive for the highest level of competence the individual can master. Here we see the importance of principle over rule. The tendency of those who favor a rule approach is to think that the professional is or is not competent. An approach based on the virtue of an ethical character requires the professional to strive toward a goal of ever-increasing mastery. One must always improve, because one never quite reaches the goal of being a complete master of the profession's expertise and skill.

Another virtue would be *fidelity*. This encompasses both loyalty and trustworthiness. The problem is to whom the fidelity is owed. It is clearly due to the client, but also to fellow professionals, and to the public interest. Obviously, serious ethical dilemmas occur when fidelity is owed in more than one direction.

The question becomes how to balance or make choices between the competing duties.

A third virtue would be *honesty*. It is hard to describe an ethical professional role that calls for dissembling or deceit, particularly to the client, fellow professionals, or those persons trusting the professional.[13] One of the serious ethical dilemmas arguably facing lawyers has been the claim often advanced that their fidelity to a particular client calls for dishonesty or dissembling to others.[14] Running counter to this is the clear obligation of the attorney not to engage in dishonesty, fraud, deceit, or misrepresentation.[15] While professionals must always be honest, they need not invariably be forthcoming or candid.

These virtues are particular in the sense of being owed to identifiable persons or institutions. Professionals are always ethically and often legally accountable for the performance of these duties to those persons. If a professional's personal character comprises competence, loyalty, and honesty, we can expand her area of discretion or autonomy without the necessity for strict monitoring.

THE PROFESSIONAL AS A SPECIAL CASE

In a different context, Ronald Dworkin has made a compelling argument about the ethical (and frequently legal) obligation of public officials to treat all members of their community as equals and to be completely impartial among them.[16] If a public official were to take the average person's normal latitude for self-preference or for favoring friends, family members, or gift givers (bribers), we would unhesitatingly describe her action as corrupt. In recent decades, we have been treated to a parade of examples from General Vaughan and Sherman Adams through to the various beneficiaries of the Department of Housing and Urban Development during the Reagan administration. Government officials have had to defend themselves against criticism about favors granted to friends or relatives that seem to defy this ethical obligation of public officials.

In contrast, we usually feel comfortable in letting private citizens, however powerful they might be, seek their own interest or make choices that favor some members of the community over others.

Clearly, professionals ought not to belong either to the class of public officials or that of private citizens. While they do bear a degree of social responsibility and public duty that we would not expect of average citizens, that responsibility does not run to an entire community as would the duty of a public official. Nor does it require impartial treatment among all the persons who would be affected by the professional's activity. In fact, the professional's obligation may require highly partial activity on behalf of some persons, most particularly the client. This is especially true of the lawyer, whose highest ethical duty is to protect the client against all other claimants or stakeholders. What is not acceptable for professionals, although it might be morally tolerable for nonprofessionals, is to seek their personal interest at the expense of the client or to prefer the interests of some other group, such as family members or wealthy friends over the interests of the client. This distinction marks an important difference between professionals and nonprofessionals.

ETHICS AND APPEARANCES

The dissonance between the requirements of high ethical conduct and the appearance of what professionals are doing is a serious component of the primary ethical dilemma. Stated differently, professionals may be required not only to act ethically, but to do so in a manner that demonstrates that fact to the public. There are three levels of occupational activity that call for different strengths of the obligation not only to maintain high ethical conduct, but its appearance as well.

The most demanding level is that of the person given authority over other human beings and their welfare. A classic example is the judge. Another is the guardian of an incompetent person. A third is the fiduciary, such as a trustee, to whom the property of another is entrusted for safekeeping. These individuals are expected to be selfless in the performance of their duties and to protect the welfare of the others for whom and to whom they are responsible. In addition, they must be seen to be selfless.

There is an interesting group of such professionals for whom the ethical dilemma may be primarily one of appearance. Administrative agencies at both the state and federal levels use hearing

officers or administrative law judges who hear applications for
benefits or conduct other hearings on behalf of their agencies.
They are civil servants and members of the bureaucracy that
employs them. At the same time, they consider themselves to
be judges and aspire to be impartial and objective. They have
adopted the Model Code of Judicial Conduct for Federal Administrative Law Judges, patterned on the Model Code of Judicial
Conduct of the American Bar Association. This Code provides
in Canon 2 that "an Administrative Law Judge should avoid
impropriety and the appearance of impropriety in all activities."[17]
And yet the structures that guarantee other judges' independence
and autonomy are not available to them. They are aware that their
role as employees of a regulatory bureaucracy where fellow employees often will appear before them as witnesses or attorneys
creates an appearance of partiality, rather than impartiality.[18]

The intermediate level of requiring the appearance of ethical
behavior contains those classes of people we exempt from social
regulation or control. Here is where the typical professional belongs. At the core of the concept of professional is the assertion
of expertise and autonomy. In its extreme form, it may be a
claim that professionals should be free from anyone, even other
professionals, looking over their shoulder. One of the strongest
claims for such freedom is made by university professors through
their professional organization, the Association of American University Professors. The 1940 Statement on Academic Freedom and
Tenure insisted on complete academic freedom for teachers and
researchers to pursue their activities, even free from control by
other professors. It provides in part:

(a) The teacher is entitled to full freedom in research and in the
publication of the results, subject to the adequate performance of his
other academic duties. . . .
(b) The teacher is entitled to freedom in the classroom in discussing
his subject, but he should be careful not to introduce into his teaching
controversial matter which has no relation to his subject. . . .
(c) The college or university teacher is a citizen, a member of a
learned profession, and an officer of an educational institution. When
he speaks or writes as a citizen, he should be free from institutional
censorship or discipline, but his special position in the community

imposes special obligations. As a man of learning and an educational officer, he should remember that the public may judge his profession and his institution by his utterances. Hence he should at all times be accurate, should exercise appropriate restraint, should show respect for the opinions of others, and should make every effort to indicate that he is not an institutional spokesman.[19]

Groups and their members can legitimately claim exemption from social and political regulation or oversight only if the freedom given them is not seriously abused. The claim that professionals should be free from supervision is most persuasive when outsiders accept that there has been little or no abuse; hence, appearances are important.

This difference in the ethical obligation to appear above reproach between the person exercising authority and the person exercising autonomy is not always understood or practiced. This is beautifully caught in Bruce Allen Murphy's appraisal of the activities of Abe Fortas shortly after he left a powerful and prestigious law practice in Washington, D.C., to become a justice of the Supreme Court of the United States:

> In reaching his determination on this matter [to serve as paid consultant to the Wolfson Foundation], Fortas made a classic mistake. He simply had not made an adjustment in ethics to fit his new circumstances. The Supreme Court, where the justices are seen by the public as unworldly monks, living like Caesar's wife, when it comes to politics and outside interests, is not the place for lawyer's briefs articulating the technical distinctions between conflict of interest and connections that in no way affect public duties and trust. This is the place for excessive concern with appearance over reality, form over substance, and figurative over the literal. Fortas, though, was still at heart a Washington lawyer who now happened to be sitting on the Supreme Court, so he could not foresee the inevitable common perception of this arrangement—a perception that by its very existence would become reality. By contracting to receive compensation for the rest of his *and his wife's* lives, Fortas made it look like any actions that he took on behalf of the *foundation* would in fact be done on behalf of *Wolfson*. And any conversations held on the problems of juveniles would automatically be assumed by the public to be conversations on Wolfson's trouble with the SEC . . . . Fortas had made himself vulnerable.[20]

The least demanding level of activity that raises the question of the relationship between ethics and appearance is the ordinary occupation, where no claim of autonomy or of trust is generally made, nor regularly acquiesced in by customers or by the public. Here, the major constraints on activity are tort rules prohibiting fraud or negligence and contractual rules imposing warranty liability. There could well be substantial regulatory activity governing how such services are performed, because the ordinary occupation has no special claim against regulatory supervision, except the general argument that the free market approach is the best way of allocating resources. Of course, many free market theorists regard all governmental or social regulation as suspect, if not downright dangerous.

For the intermediate category, in which the professions are located, the problem now is often the reverse of that facing Justice Fortas. Instead of being concerned about whether they meet the higher level of apparent ethical conduct demanded in the first category, the professions' concern ought to be whether the appearance or reputation of the profession has sunk so low that individual clients or the public perceive no difference between the professions and the third level of ordinary occupations, in which case the claim to autonomy and freedom from supervision becomes unpersuasive.

THE PROFESSIONAL CODES

The obligation to provide only those services that are necessary can be derived from the nature of the relationship between the professional counsellor or professional service provider and the client, as well as from the role of the competent professional. Professional ethical codes might then be seen as merely formalizing or memorializing this duty. Codes could also restrict or limit the duty. To the extent that an ethical code does not explicitly mention the duty, states it ambiguously, or weakens the injunction, it is always open to those professionals tempted to pursue self-interest rather than the welfare of their clients to make a legalistic argument that literal compliance with the provisions of the code is all that professional ethics requires.

The formal ethical codes adopted by the various professions may be viewed from a number of different, sometimes critical, perspectives. One way is to see the codes as catalogs of ethical problems identified by either the profession or client complaints. Another is to view a code as a codification and a formal adoption of ethical attitudes and practices that evolved over time. A code could also be thought of as a public relations document, drafted by the profession to persuade the public that its members are in fact ethical. The code may be viewed as an instrument of monopoly and control designed to exclude from the area of professional activity all who do not subscribe to the code.[21] Finally, it may be viewed as a set of rules, compliance with which makes the professional ethical. Of course, it can be considered to be just what it purports to be, a code of ethics setting forth the expectations of behavior by which the professional will be judged by clients, by fellow professionals, and by the public.

The analysis of this book is generated by the belief that most practicing professionals take the codes seriously as a set of ethical guidelines, so that failure to comply not merely with the letter, but the spirit of the code, produces psychological guilt. Whether there is legal or ethical guilt in an objective sense turns on the resolution of the issues that I am considering.

In examining the codes of professional ethics and the form in which the propositions are stated, it is important to note whether the statements appear more like ethical standards or like sets of legal prescriptions. The distinguishing characteristics are of two kinds. One is the level of generality or specificity. The other is the type of sanctions envisioned. If the profession intends to use the code as a basis for imposing sanctions, then it become quasi-law, if not clearly law. The sanction of reprimand is more consistent with an ethical system, while the sanctions of suspension or revocation of license are more like legal sanctions.

In the following material, I want to look at selections from some sample professional codes to see (1) the extent to which they recognize the dilemma posed in this book as a problem, (2) how explicitly they adopt formal guidelines to deal with the problem, (3) how much help they offer the individual professional in trying to balance and resolve the competing pressures, (4) whether their prescriptions and sanctions are more like ethical injunctions or legal rules, and finally (5) in what ways the context and pressures differ among the various professions.

The Legal Profession

Canon 5 of The American Bar Association's Model Code of Professional Responsibility prescribes that "A Lawyer Should Exercise Independent Professional Judgment on Behalf of a Client"[22] and Ethical Consideration 5-1 further elaborates this by providing:

> The professional judgment of a lawyer should be exercised, within the bounds of the law, solely for the benefit of his client and free of compromising influences and loyalties. Neither his personal interests, the interests of other clients, nor the desires of third persons should be permitted to dilute his loyalty to his client.[23]

This is not quite explicit about the question of providing unnecessary services, but the prohibition is clearly implicit. The lawyer as a matter of professional ethics must subordinate his own interest to that of the client; that is, she should consider only the best interests of her client.[24]

Among all professionals, the lawyer has the fewest problems of formal role conflict. The classic view of lawyers is that they are the champions and representatives of their clients, and their loyalty should be undivided. It is this view that makes the provision of excessive services so obviously inappropriate and perhaps explains why a member of the legal profession would be more likely to focus on this dilemma. The problem does not disappear for other professionals, but given the ways in which other professionals are embedded in multiple roles, the resolution of the dilemma becomes more complex.

The legal profession seems to be in the process of moving from the aspirational statements found in the Model Code of Professional Responsibility to a much more rule-oriented approach. The American Bar Association adopted the Model Rules of Professional Conduct in 1983. They are much more detailed and specific than the Canons of the Model Code. Rules most pertinent to the dilemma discussed here are:

RULE 1.1   COMPETENCE

A lawyer shall provide competent representation to a client. Competent representation requires the legal knowledge, skill, thoroughness and preparation reasonably necessary for the representation.

RULE 1.7   CONFLICT OF INTEREST: GENERAL RULE . . .

(b) A lawyer shall not represent a client if the representation of that client may be materially limited by the lawyer's responsibilities to another client or to a third person, or by the lawyer's own interests, unless:

> (1) the lawyer reasonably believes the representation will not be adversely affected; and
> (2) the client consents after consultation. When representation of multiple clients in a single matter is undertaken, the consultation shall include explanation of the implications of the common representation and the advantages and risks involved.

Comment to RULE 1.7
Lawyer's Interests

[6] The lawyer's own interest should not be permitted to have adverse effect on representation of a client. For example, a lawyer's need for income should not lead the lawyer to undertake matters that cannot be handled competently and at a reasonable fee. See Rules 1.1 and 1.5. If the probity of a lawyer's own conduct in a transaction is in serious question, it may be difficult or impossible for the lawyer to give a client detached advice. A lawyer may not allow related business interests to affect representation, for example, by referring clients to an enterprise in which the lawyer has an undisclosed interest.

Even in these more specific rules, the prohibition against providing unnecessary services is implicit, rather than explicit.

The Medical Profession

The doctor is bound by the Hippocratic oath or its modern variants to a similar ethical obligation, that is, to only perform those services necessary to promote and maintain the patient's health.

The American Medical Association's Principles of Medical Ethics provide in part:

PREAMBLE:
The medical profession has long subscribed to a body of ethical statements developed primarily for the benefit of the patient. As a member of this profession, a physician must recognize responsibility not only to patients, but also to society, to other health professionals, and to self. The following Principles adopted by the American Medical Association are not laws, but standards of conduct which define the essentials of honorable behavior for the physician.

I. A physician shall be dedicated to providing competent medical service with compassion and respect for human dignity.

II. A physician shall deal honestly with patients and colleagues, and strive to expose those physicians deficient in character or competence, or who engage in fraud or deception.

V. A physician shall continue to study, apply and advance scientific knowledge, make relevant information available to patients, colleagues, and the public, obtain consultation, and use the talents of other health professionals when indicated.

The requirements that physicians provide competent medical services, deal honestly with patients and make relevant information available to patients, and expose physicians engaged in fraud or deception all strongly imply prohibition against providing unnecessary services in order to increase the physician's income at the expense of the patient and the patient's needs. This is made quite explicit in more specific ethical principles:

2.16   UNNECESSARY SERVICES
It is unethical for a physician to provide or prescribe unnecessary services or unnecessary ancillary facilities. (II, VII)

2.17   WORTHLESS SERVICES
A physician should not seek compensation for providing services which he knows or should know are generally regarded among reputable physicians as worthless. (II, VII)[25]

It is interesting to note the degree to which the medical profession stresses, in contrast with the law, that every physician performs as a member of a system of other health care professionals, and that ethical obligations are therefore owed to those other professionals. Medicine is very much a cooperative profession, whereas law is frequently an adversarial one. Difficult ethical conflicts can arise when the duty owed to a fellow professional conflicts with the duty owed to the patient. The medical code recognizes this possibility more explicitly, but does not give much, if any, guidance either on the strengths or weights of these various obligations, or on how a conflict should be resolved. If the general injunction that a professional must protect or prefer the interests of the client is very weighty, then this conflict should normally be resolved by preferring the interests of the client over those of fellow professionals. In fact, many professionals believe that their relationships with other professionals are so important to the continued practice of their professions that the conflicts are often resolved the other way.[26]

Nursing

Nursing has special problems that need to be specified before we go to the code. Its striving for professional status came fairly recently, much later than the dominant and prestigious profession of medicine. Historically, nurses were a subordinate profession to medical doctors. Doctors made the decisions about health care and nurses executed their decisions and followed their prescriptions. Both doctor and nurse worked together as a team, but it was clear who was the director of the team. Nurses today occupy an intermediate position among the professionals and other employees in a health care situation. According to Abbott:

Since doctors dominate the medical division of labor, they invoke their clear *public* relations [dominant position of jurisdiction] with everyone else in the hospital. Nurses, on the other hand, emphasize their formal separation from *their* subordinates, but emphasize, vis-à-vis physicians, the functions and knowledge that both groups share.[27]

The Nursing Code of Ethics contains a strong claim for being accepted as professionals, a not very hidden claim for more autonomy from medical doctors than has traditionally been given them. There is also an understanding that their serious ethical problems arise out of their assistance to and cooperation with medical doctors. The difficulties nurses face in their subordinate role are often those of the whistle-blower. When does their concern for the welfare of the patient require them to protect him by calling attention to incompetent or unethical practices of other health care professionals with whom they are working as a team? This raises ethical dilemmas of much greater complexity than those faced by such clearly autonomous professionals as doctors and lawyers.

The drafters of the Nursing Code of Ethics could draw on the experience of many other professions in developing formal codes. Their code is well drafted not only in justifying the position of nursing as a profession and in grounding ethics in something other than authoritative rules, but in identifying the serious ethical problems faced by nurses.

INTRODUCTION

A code of ethics indicates a profession's acceptance of the responsibility and trust with which it has been invested by society. Under the terms of the implicit contract between society and the nursing profession, society grants the profession considerable autonomy and authority to function in the conduct of its affairs. The development of a code of ethics is an essential activity of a profession and provides one means for the exercise of professional self-regulation.

Upon entering the profession, each nurse inherits a measure of both the responsibility and the trust that have accrued to nursing over the years, as well as the corresponding obligation to adhere to the profession's code of conduct and relationships for ethical practice. . . .

CODE FOR NURSES

1. The nurse provides services with respect for human dignity and the uniqueness of the client, unrestricted by considerations of social or economic status, personal attributes, or the nature of health problems.

2. The nurse safeguards the client's right to privacy by judiciously protecting information of a confidential nature.

3. The nurse acts to safeguard the client and the public when health care and safety are affected by the incompetent, unethical, or illegal practice of any person.

4. The nurse assumes responsibility and accountability for individual nursing judgments and actions.

5. The nurse maintains competence in nursing.

6. The nurse exercises informed judgment and uses individual competence and qualifications as criteria in seeking consultation, accepting responsibilities, and delegating nursing activities to others. . . .

10. The nurse participates in the profession's efforts to protect the public from misinformation and misrepresentation and to maintain the integrity of nursing.

11. The nurse collaborates with members of the health professions and other citizens in promoting community and national efforts to meet the health needs of the public.[28]

That part of the code that deals explicitly with the nurses' problems as whistle-blower will be discussed in Chapter 7.

Public Accounting

Not all accountants are public accountants. Many are employed by businesses and other clients to keep their financial records and prepare financial reports. The relationship between a client and an in-house accountant is strictly one of employment, and usually does not raise the professional's ethical dilemmas. The in-house accountant, of course, may face ethical quandaries when asked to make false entries, such as recording an employer's personal expenses as business expenses. The danger is that the employer may use his financial records not only internally, but to influence the actions of the public, such as investors or lenders, or to mislead governmental officials, such as taxing authorities. These outsiders will not accept the validity of self-prepared financial statements. That is where the profession of public accounting becomes critical.

The responsibility of a public accountant is to make audits and certify that the financial reports prepared by clients are truthful and honest. These reports are relied on by members of the general public either to invest money in the business or to lend money to the client. Thus the accountant has a duty to the client who will be paying his bill, but also a duty to the public that the audit and certification can be relied on.

RULES OF CONDUCT OF THE CODE OF PROFESSIONAL ETHICS OF THE AMERICAN INSTITUTION OF PUBLIC ACCOUNTANTS

RULE 101—INDEPENDENCE

A member of a firm of which he is a partner or shareholder shall not express an opinion on financial statements of an enterprise unless he and his firm are independent with respect to such enterprise.

RULE 102—INTEGRITY AND OBJECTIVITY

A member shall not knowingly misinterpret facts and when engaged in the practice of public accounting, including the rendering of tax and management advisory services, shall not subordinate his judgment to others. In tax practice, a member may resolve doubt in favor of his client as long as there is reasonable support for his position.

RULE 201—GENERAL STANDARDS

A member shall comply with the following general standards as interpreted by bodies designated by Council and must justify any departures therefrom.

A. *Professional competence.* A member shall undertake only those engagements which he or his firm can reasonably expect to complete with professional competence.

B. *Due professional care.* A member shall exercise due professional care in the performance of an engagement.

C. *Planning and supervision.* A member shall adequately plan and supervise an engagement.

D. *Sufficient relevant data.* A member shall obtain sufficient relevant data to afford a reasonable basis for conclusions or recommendations in relation to an engagement.

E. *Forecasts.* A member shall not permit his name to be used in conjunction with any forecast of future transactions in a manner which may lead to the belief that the member vouches for the achievability of the forecast.

RULE 302—CONTINGENT FEES

Professional services shall not be offered or rendered under an arrangement whereby no fee will be charged unless a specified finding or result is attained, or where the fee is otherwise contingent upon the findings or results of such services.

RULE 504—INCOMPATIBLE OCCUPATIONS

A member who is engaged in the practice of public accounting shall not concurrently engage in any business or occupation which would create a conflict of interest in rendering professional services.[29]

What is clear from this code is that public accountants are primarily concerned with the objectivity, honesty, and reliability of their reports. The temptation they are subject to is not the furnishing of unnecessary services, but dishonest or untruthful statements. To this end, there is great concern about conflicts of interest or financial incentives that would pressure toward this violation. There is also a concern that the accountant not perform sloppily or go into areas where she does not have the requisite training or experience. This is an ethical problem all professionals face, but many codes are not as explicit about the unethical quality of slipshod performance.

Independent Insurance Agents

The National Association of Insurance Agents, a group that in 1973 represented 31,000 independent insurance agencies and approximately 150,000 individual insurance agents, adopted a Code of Ethics for its members in 1929. It provides in part:

I believe in the insurance business and its future, and that the American agent is the instrumentality through which it reaches its highest point and attains its widest distribution.

I will do my part to uphold and upbuild the American Agency System which has developed insurance to its present fundamental place in the economic fabric of our nation, and to my fellow-members of the National Association of Insurance Agents I pledge myself always to support right principles and oppose bad practices in the business.

I believe that these three have their distinct rights in our business: first, the Public; second, the Insurance Companies; and third, the Insurance Agents; and that the rights of the Public are paramount.

To the Public

I regard the insurance business as an honorable profession and realize that it affords me a distinct opportunity to serve society.

I will strive to render the full measure of service that should be expected from an intelligent, well-informed insurance man. Anything short of this would be a violation of the trust imposed in me.

I will thoroughly analyze the insurance needs of my clients and recommend the forms of indemnity best suited to these needs, faithfully advising as to the best insurance protection available.

The rhetoric of this code has a very different tone from those of professions like law and medicine. Those professional codes seem quite clearly to address only the members of the profession and to give them ethical guidelines. This code appears to be addressed as much or more to people outside the profession as to independent insurance agents. To other professionals, the claim is that insurance agents are truly professionals; to members of the general public, the code asserts that agents are more than just business people and thus are as trustworthy as other professionals. It has a clear public relations function.

The independent insurance agent is really a broker or intermediary, a person who brings together the customer who needs insurance with an insurance company. The independent agent is clearly not an employee of either and owes duties of loyalty to both. In a role analysis, this professional has two clients, whose interests are often in conflict. This has caused numerous problems for the courts, when the relationship between insured and insurer goes sour, because of some activity of the insurance agent. The courts are faced with difficult problems of whether the independent agent was acting as an agent for the insurance company or for the insurance customer.[30] The determination of this issue may be decisive of the controversy between insured and insurer, because the principal is legally responsible for the activities of the agent.

In addressing the professional's dilemma, this Code is quite explicit on two fundamental points. The agent owes a duty to the client to recommend the insurance best suited to the client's needs and to advise faithfully on the best insurance protection available. If this duty conflicts with any obligation to insurance companies or fellow agents, the protection of the client is primary. Although it does not address the self-interest of the agent himself in so many words, it is quite clear that the injunction to recommend insurance best suited to the client's needs equally requires subordination of the interest of the agent.

Other Professions

It is equally plausible to impose on other professional occupations, such as architects, stockbrokers, and engineers, an ethical obligation to promote and protect the client's interest over the self-interest of the professional.

If we look at the five professions and their codes as examples demonstrating the variety of ethical problems faced by the professions, we can see they differ on several axes or lines of reference one; the degree of autonomy enjoyed by the professional, another, the complexity of the role relationships the professional is involved in, and finally, the prestige enjoyed by the profession. This is an apparent correlation among the various professions' places on the several axes. The more prestigious the profession, the more autonomy and the less complex role conflicts its members enjoy. This is not surprising, because duties owed to more than one other right-holder are a constraint on autonomy. As one moves along these axes, the ethical problems change, both in type and in quality. Clearly, only those professionals with substantial prestige, proclaimed expertise, and autonomy can choose to abuse their positions by providing excessive or unnecessary services (at least without easy detection). As one goes down the prestige axis to professional groups with less autonomy and more complex role responsibilities, the ethical dilemma is more that of the whistle-blower, the one who must call to the attention of the authorities or the public when there has been abuse of ethical discretion by more powerful professionals. It is not an accident that many of the toughest ethical dilemmas are actually borne by those with the least prestige and power. What value is there in prestige and power if they cannot be used to make life easier?

SUMMARY

One defining characteristic of a profession is the adoption of a code of ethics.[31] A code of ethics may be seen as a collection of rules, in which case the professional's ethical obligation is merely to comply with the minimum requirements stated by the rules. If the code is viewed as a collection of rules, its precepts are often drafted in such a way that the application of the obligation of a professional to always prefer the interests of the client may be unclear in particular cases. Codes could be viewed as designed to control the way members of the profession cooperate with each other and to obligate them to protect the territory of the profession from encroachment by competitors. Codes may be perceived as public relations documents aimed at the general public to persuade them that professionals are more than self-interested profit seekers and can be trusted to give good advice and disinterested service. I feel that most professionals take the codes more seriously than these critical analyses imply. If so, they feel guilt or remorse when acting in ways inconsistent with the letter or the spirit of the code.

Professional ethics can also be analyzed as a set of principles, attitudes, or types of character dispositions that should control the way the profession is practiced. The purpose of the adoption of a formal code, then, is to force professionals to be aware of ethical responsibilities and to develop an ethical attitude or orientation. It is in this latter sense that I prefer to use the term *professional ethics*. A distinguishing characteristic of a profession as contrasted with an occupation is that the professional is expected to act differently from a business person in dealing with clients. The professional is there to serve the client, not merely to make money. If this is to be more than a rationalization justifying a professional monopoly of an area of expertise, the relationship between professional and client must be one of trust, not the arms-length transaction of the market. Inside such a relationship, the provision of unnecessary services clearly violates the fiduciary responsibilities of the professional.

If it is clear what professionals ought to do, but they are not doing it, there must be a reason. The explanation is that there is a powerful competing goal to make money and achieve social status. Whether we describe this choice between service or success as an ethical dilemma depends largely on whether we include compliance problems in the field of ethics.

If everyone agrees on what the ethical standard should be, but it is frequently not followed, what should happen? In trying to eliminate or minimize the dilemma for actual practicing professionals, I want in the latter chapters of the book to consider five options:

1. Redefining the ethical obligation
2. Requiring an informed consent after the client is told not only about the factors going into the professional judgment, but also about the ethical dilemma itself
3. Restructuring professional institutions and practices so the dilemma will be minimized or eliminated.
4. Compelling compliance with ethical norms by law
5. Requiring professional schools and organizations to sufficiently educate, reinforce, and monitor professionals so they will be strongly motivated to comply.

The one option I find unacceptable, but which may well be the current stance of the professions, is to pretend the problem does not exist, or is minimal. As H.L.A. Hart said in another context:

Surely if we have learned anything from the history of morals it is that the thing to do with a moral quandary is not to hide it. Like nettles, the occasions when life forces us to choose between the lesser of two evils must be grasped with the consciousness that they are what they are.[32]

NOTES

1. In *The Oxford English Dictionary*, vol. 3 (Oxford: Clarendon Press, 1969), 312, *Ethics* is defined as "3. In narrower sense, with some qualifying word or phrase; a. The moral principles or system of a particular leader or school of thought. . . . b. The moral principles by which a person is guided. . . . c. The rules of conduct recognized in certain associations or departments of human life."
2. This view of market ethics is that it is the duty of each buyer to protect himself and there is no obligation on any seller to look out for the welfare of a buyer. It is frequently summarized by the Latin phrase *caveat emptor*.
3. Alasdair MacIntyre, *After Virtue* (Notre Dame, Ind.: University of Notre Dame Press, 1981), 18.
4. This dilemma is similar to the one discussed in detail in Chapter 7.

5. See discussion in Chapter 9.

6. MacIntyre, *After Virtue*, 112.

7. Ronald Dworkin, *Taking Rights Seriously* (Cambridge, Mass.: Harvard University Press, 1978), 22:

> I just spoke of 'principles, policies, and other sorts of standards'. Most often I shall use the term 'principle' to refer to the whole set of these standards other than rules; occasionally, however, I shall be more precise, and distinguish between principles and policies. . . . I call a 'policy' that kind of standard that sets out a goal to be reached, generally an improvement in some economic, political, or social feature of the community. . . . I call a 'principle' a standard that is to be observed, not because it will advance or secure an economic, political, or social situation deemed desirable, but because it is a requirement of justice or fairness or some other dimension of morality.

8. Where the ellipses occur, I omitted the qualifier "legal" from the quote. While Dworkin is talking about legal systems and obligations, the distinction strikes me as equally valid for ethical systems.

9. Dworkin, *Taking Rights Seriously*, 24.

10. Ibid, 26.

11. See the discussion in Chapter 4.

12. Many professional codes of ethics specifically require the professional to be competent, but do not specify the level of competence that ought to be attained. For lawyers, see the American Bar Association's Model Code of Professional Responsibility Canon 6: "A Lawyer Should Represent a Client Competently"; for doctors, see the American Medical Association's Principles of Medical Ethics, Preamble, I; for public accountants, see Code of Professional Ethics of the American Institution of Public Accounts, Rule 201 A; and for nurses, see Code for Nurses, 5. The provisions of these code sections are set forth verbatim later in this chapter.

13. An often-discussed exception to this proposition is the purported obligation of a medical doctor to not disclose the nature of some illnesses to a client if the knowledge would be psychologically disturbing. See extended discussion in Sissela Bok, *Lying: Moral Choice in Public and Private Life* (New York: Vintage Books, 1978), 232–55.

14. This is often defended as required by Canon 4 of the Model Code of Professional Responsibility: "A Lawyer Should Preserve the Confidences and Secrets of a Client." A well-known recent controversy over the application of this principle concerned the attorneys representing Robert Garrow, who was being prosecuted for murder

in New York. In the course of preparing for trial, Garrow told them that he had committed previous murders and where he had buried the bodies. To check his veracity, the attorneys found the bodies. They did not report the location of the bodies until after the trial, even though the families of the victims were desperately seeking information about their whereabouts. As would be expected, this outraged the families as well as a substantial majority of the newspaper-reading public. For a discussion see Barry S. Martin, "The Garrow Case Revisited: A Lesson for the Serial Murderer's Counsel," *Criminal Justice Journal* (1987): 197.

15. See American Bar Association, *Model Code of Professional Responsibility*, Disciplinary Rule 1-102(A)(4).

16. Ronald Dworkin, *Law's Empire* (Cambridge, Mass.: Harvard University Press, 1986), 173–75.

17. American Bar Association, *Model Code of Judicial Conduct for Federal Administrative Law Judges*, 1989, 3.

18. This was made very clear to me by both public statements and private comments made after I addressed the Annual Conference of the National Association of Administrative Law Judges held in Kansas City in October, 1990, on the subject of the professional's dilemma.

19. American Association of University Professors, *Policy Documents & Reports*, 1984 ed., 3–4.

20. Bruce Allen Murphy, *Fortas: The Rise and Ruin of a Supreme Court Justice* (New York: William Morrow & Co., 1988), 198–99.

21. Andrew Abbott, *The System of Professions: An Essay on the Division of Expert Labor* (Chicago: University of Chicago Press, 1988), 5:

> For the new theorists, the regularity of professionalization was not the visible regularity of school, then association, then ethics code, but rather the hidden one of successive functions for these professional forms. Ethics codes came late in professionalization not because they were a culmination of natural growth, but because they served the function of excluding outsiders, a function that became important only after the professional community had been generated and consolidated. Since ethics codes did not serve these earlier functions, they came late.

22. American Bar Association, Model Code of Professional Responsibility, Canon 5 (as amended August 1980), 24.

23. Ibid.

24. In *Crisci v. Security Insurance Co.*, 66 Cal.2d 425, 426 P.2d 173 (1967), the Supreme Court of California in considering an analogous problem, the duty of an insurance company attorney hired by a liability insurance company to represent the insured, said that "the insurer must

give the interests of the insured at least as much consideration as it gives to its own interest; and that when 'there is great risk of a recovery beyond the policy limits so that the most reasonable manner of disposing of the claim is a settlement which can be made within those limits, a consideration in good faith of the insured's interest requires the insurer to settle the claim.' " (From *Comunale v. Traders and General Ins. Co.*, 50 Cal.2d 654 at 659, 328 P.2d 201, 1958.)

25. Rena A. Gorlin, ed., *Codes of Professional Responsibility* (Washington, D.C.: Bureau of National Affairs, 1986), 109.

26. While not formally recognized, this is a problem also faced by lawyers. See discussion at the end of this chapter's section on role conflicts, above.

27. See Abbott, *The System of Professions*, 67.

28. Ibid, 151–58.

29. Taken from Gorlin, *Codes of Professional Responsibility*, 237–41.

30. For a more detailed discussion of this problem, including citation to cases, see Robert E. Keeton and Alan I. Widiss, *Insurance Law*, Student ed. (St. Paul: West Publishing Co., 1988), §2.5(d), 100.

31. Abbott, *The System of Professions*, 4:

Carr-Saunders and Wilson's *The Professions*, published in 1934 . . . gave historical background on every group that could then be considered a profession in England. Its theoretical discussion systematized a view of professions that had by then come to dominate the writings both of the professions themselves and of the social scientists examining them. Professions were organized bodies of experts who applied esoteric knowledge to particular cases. They had elaborate systems of instruction and training, together with entry by examination and other formal prerequisites. They normally possessed and enforced a code of ethics or behavior. This list of properties became the core of later definitions.

32. H.L.A. Hart, "Positivism and the Separation of Law and Morals," *Harvard Law Review* 71 (1958): 619–20.

4

The Pressure for Financial Success

If it is clear what professionals ethically ought to do, but they are not doing it, an explanation must be sought. It lies with a powerful competing goal—success, whether by making money, attaining a prestigious status, having the ability to exercise power, or attaining a high level of economic security. In an ideal world, a person ought to choose a profession as a vocation, as a means of serving others, as a commitment to public service, rather than for extrinsic rewards, such as money, power, security, or prestige. In America, few have chosen to become professionals solely from idealistic motives, although the tradition is that at least teachers, clergy, and social workers do so. Most choose for a mix of internal and external rewards, and a great many applicants for the professions are interested only in the extrinsic rewards.[1]

It is important to distinguish between formal ethical positions to which nominal allegiance is given and the real rules of conduct governing actual choices made by people. At this second level, one might argue that social mores, with acquiescence from professional organizations, have seriously eroded professional ethical rules in a way that minimizes the dilemma by tolerating, if not legitimating, the pursuit of financial self-interest. Stated differently, there is the formal ethical prescription that a professional must prefer the interest of the client, as well as the currently accepted primary goal of all economic or business activity, which is to make as much profit as possible.

The dilemma appears as a choice between two ends or aims of professional life. In daily situations, professionals must decide how much weight to give each aim as balances are drawn in real contexts of professional judgment. In large urban communities, the balance is being struck differently than it once was in smaller, tightly-knit communities. This trend is obvious when one compares the very large urban law firm with the small general practice firm in a moderate-sized town, or the hospital corporation run for profit with the old nonprofit governmental hospitals. In complex, modern, profit-oriented professional groupings, the business imperative of keeping costs down and income high, often pushed by nonprofessional[2] business managers, tends to overwhelm nonprofit, public service activities, except those undertaken for high-profile public relations, such as the requirement of many law firms that their associates do a limited amount of *pro bono* work.

One might argue that the two drives toward service to the client and toward financial success are not necessarily contradictory in practice. It would seem almost axiomatic that the way to retain and control clients is to give them competent and honest service, which protects their welfare. For the self-employed independent practitioner, as well as for professionals in large organizations, keeping clients satisfied so they will return for and insist on the services of this particular professional seems the best way to guarantee financial success and improved social esteem.[3]

The problem is that competent and honest service need not be the reality, but only must seem so to the client. Many clients can judge only with great difficulty whether their interests have really been served by the professional's technical expertise. Clients are heavily dependent on the advice given and the evaluation made by the professional whose conduct is in question. This encourages manipulation of the client to make him feel as though he is well served. This is particularly apt to be the result if rendering the services that the client has been manipulated to believe are satisfactory costs the professional less than delivering true service, but can be billed or presented at the rate of the true service.

THE PRESSURE FOR FINANCIAL SUCCESS

When one moves below formal ethical rules to a more realistic level of ethics to determine the aims or moral principles that work in people's consciences, one must look carefully for evidence. I assume that the formal ethical guideline requiring a professional to prefer her client's interests is not just nominal for most professionals. On the other hand, it is not so powerful that it always carries the field. I want to discuss four factors guiding professional success: (1) the competitiveness of getting into the professions, (2) the rapidly escalating cost of professional education, which requires substantial financial success to justify the investment, (3) the cultural attitude that measures social and professional success largely in terms of material income, and (4) the legitimation of the increased use of advertising by leading professions like law and medicine.

Competition to Enter the Profession

The competitiveness required to get into the professions creates a mind-set of the necessity of being better than others, both inside the profession and among other members of society. In this society, we are introduced to competition long before we begin formal schooling. Alfie Kohn defines the structural competition we are socialized to accept and participate in this way:

> To say that an activity is structurally competitive is to say that it is characterized by what I call mutually exclusive goal attainment ("MEGA" for short). This means very simply, that my success requires your failure. Our fates are negatively linked. If one of us must lose exactly as much as the other wins, as in poker, then we are talking about a "zero-sum game." But in any MEGA arrangement, two or more individuals are trying to achieve a goal that cannot be achieved by all of them. This is the essence of competition.[4]

Professions offer their members more prestige and income than most nonprofessional jobs. Among the professions, some are more prestigious and financially rewarding than others. Inside each profession, there are specialties and locations of practice that are more desirable. Young people in secondary school who are ambitious will be advised or will think about where in this hierarchy they would like to be placed for their occupational (and social) life. The more desirable the profession or the more prestigious the professional school, the more competitive will be the admissions process and the subsequent struggle for high class standing. This is, of course, training for what will be a very competitive professional world in which students must perform for the rest of their working lives. Throughout this professional socialization, the young professional, along with everyone else, is being conditioned to separate her colleagues into "winners" and "losers." Our highest accolades are reserved for winners; losers receive pity at best, contempt at worst. However much one personally dislikes this evaluative system, everyone who receives a professional education in this country is trapped within its values.

The Cost of Professional Education

The high and rapidly escalating cost of professional education requires very substantial financial success to justify economically the decision to enter the profession. When the cost of professional education runs into the tens of thousands of dollars and recent graduates carry large student loan obligations,[5] aspiring professionals cannot be indifferent or blasé about the compensation they are to receive after graduation.

This has been a particular problem in both law and medicine. The young lawyer who is idealistic and committed most strongly to public service rather than mere financial success would in the past have chosen public service practice, such as becoming a public defender or a legal aid lawyer. These jobs tend to pay salaries so modest that graduates with large student loans or other responsibilities such as dependent families cannot afford to take them. Idealistic young doctors who might be attracted to general practice in rural communities or to working in poor neighborhoods may also be priced out of those options because of the debt they created during their extended and expensive period of professional training.

Professional educators who have a commitment to professional ethics and who encourage students to have a commitment to working for the public good are dismayed by how quickly almost all students, aware of these financial realities, dismiss their appeal.

The Cultural Emphasis on Material Success

The preceding two sections discuss competitive and financial factors that are created by and within the professions and professional education. We are all, however, not merely members of professions, but also members of the total culture. To the extent that we aspire to attain social prestige and respect in the larger society, we must satisfy the criteria that are held widely through the entire society. The cultural attitude displayed incessantly in the mass media is that material success, with all the accompanying prerogatives, is the most important achievement. That attitude was always present in our society, but has been even more dominant in the last two decades.

Increased Use of Professional Advertising

The legitimation of the use of advertising by the prestigious professions of law and medicine exacerbates the competitiveness and the pressure for financial success. Advertising increases the cost of professional activity, which then requires more income to cover the cost of advertising and to improve take-home profits. This can fairly be termed a vicious circle. It would be hard to say whether the increased use of advertising is the result of competitiveness and scarcity of employment, or is a cause of increased competitiveness. Expanded advertising swells the cost of services to the client, unless the advertising increases business. If the service would not be sought by the client without the advertising, this raises vexing questions about how necessary the service really was. Even in its present form, professional advertising may bring to the attention of sectors of the public that are traditionally underserved that there are experts who can help with their problems.

The probable motivation of advertisers is to get a larger market share for the advertiser by diverting customers from their present providers. The market share analysis assumes a relatively stable demand and an oversupply of professionals competing for those customers.

Advertising traditionally has been defended as a means of giving consumers information so they can make wise choices among the options offered by the market. However, in a situation where the factors of choice are as complex as they are for determining the abilities of professional providers, the typical advertisement gives little information on which to make sound choices.

Some social and economic critics contend that the real function of advertising is to increase demand by creating wants that do not presently exist.[6] As stated by John Kultgen, "Our perception of our needs is not always correct. Where an occupational group has aggressively publicized its services, demand may reflect false consciousness and false needs or an indulgence of the wants of some at the expense of the needs of others."[7] This has happened in law, in medicine, in the insurance industry, as well as in many other professional occupations. Lawsuits are brought today that would not have been filed without the influence of lawyer advertising.[8] The medical industry has been successful in promoting the widespread use of many drugs, particularly sedatives and pain killers, as well as in encouraging new procedures of questionable necessity, like cosmetic surgery. The insurance industry, through advertising, has increased both the types and amount of insurance that most consumers purchase.

Thus, advertising is both produced by and then contributes to the drive of professionals to be financially successful.

INCOME AS AN INDEX TO PRESTIGE
AND SUCCESS

From the professional's viewpoint, the demands for ethical performance and the pressures for social and financial success create a very real human, if not ethical, conflict. She understands she should give the client sound counsel or advice without regard to her own gain or loss. At the same time, she has been socialized into thinking she must be successful as a professional and that success is measured by how much professional income she receives.[9] At the upper reaches of the professions, where the provider is assured sufficient income so that prudent earners would say that additional revenue is not essential, the pressures are those of a competitive society, that is, to be always better than competitors.[10] From the time of entrance into the professions, the student and later the professional is conditioned to compete. Entrance into any profession is somewhat competitive, as many members of the society do not meet even the minimal qualifications to enter training programs. Among the professions, there is a status or hierarchy of prestige, so that public school teachers, nurses, and accountants enjoy less prestige, less autonomy, and less income than university professors, doctors, and lawyers. At the upper end of the pyramid, each profession is much more competitive, so that one starts by trying to get into the most prestigious professional school. Once inside that school, one tries to be the best of one's contemporaries. Upon graduation and licensing, one tries to get the most prestigious and remunerative entry position; and throughout one's professional career, one tries to be the most successful. Pecking order places are notoriously hard to define and highly subjective. One needs an index to be sure of place. In professional school, it is grades. Past the licensing period, it is material things such as titles, office or work prerogatives, and income. When ranking or trying to determine places, the ultimate index to success is probably professional income because it is quantified in a way that prestige or power cannot be.

The most successful professionals are in general least subject to direct economic pressures to act unethically. Once they obtain the reputation for being among the most competent and able of their professional group, they are inundated with clients and requests for service. They can refuse any business that requires sharp practice or unethical behavior. Since these highly successful practitioners also often serve as leaders and spokespersons for the profession, they, based on their own experience, downplay the existence of the dilemma.

Even the most successful and altruistic professionals cannot always escape the problems of competitive pressure. Due to an

increase in the number of surgeons as well as new medical therapies that are enjoying great success against diseases that previously required open surgery, there is an erosion of the number of
opportunities for surgeons to operate.[11] This has unpleasant consequences not only for surgeons, but often for patients. Surgeons
are either pressured to perform unnecessary surgery or to move
into other specialties, such as internal medicine. If they avoid
either of these undesirable alternatives, they perform too few
operations to keep their surgical skills at their peak. None of these
options is desirable for an ethical, well-trained, and competent
surgeon.

As one goes down the scale toward marginal providers of professional services, the economic compulsions are different and
perhaps stronger. There is overhead expense, such as rent, equipment, support personnel, and liability insurance, in the operation
of any profession. There is an inelastic need for income sufficient
not only to cover these business expenses, but to support oneself
and one's dependents. For marginal professionals with serious
cash flow problems who do not see enough clients anyway, the
temptation to perform unnecessary services for those who find
their way into the office may be hard to resist.

For those professionals who are subordinates or who are employed in large bureaucratic organizations, the success pressures
may have a different quality. They often do not seek autonomy
and opportunity to expand their income, prestige, and power.
They may instead be risk-averse and interested in economic security. For these professionals, the possibility that they may lose
their jobs, be demoted, or miss an opportunity for advancement
inside the organization can be a very powerful motivation impelling them to act unethically by providing unnecessary services
to clients or by acquiescing in such activity being done by their
organization.

THE PRIMARY SUCCESS GOAL

Is the pressure along the success horn of the dilemma primarily pressure for financial success, for achieving social status and
esteem, or for attaining power? Karl Polanyi argues:

[T]here is the equally mistaken doctrine of the essentially economic nature of class interests. Though human society is naturally conditioned by economic factors, the motives of human individuals are only exceptionally determined by the needs of material want-satisfaction. That nineteenth century society was organized on the assumption that such a motivation could be made universal was a peculiarity of the age. It was therefore appropriate to allow a comparatively wide scope to the play of economic motives when analyzing that society. But we must guard against prejudging the issue, which is precisely to what extent such an unusual motivation could be made effective.

Purely economic matters such as affect want-satisfaction are incomparably less relevant to class behavior than questions of social recognition. Want-satisfaction may be, of course, the result of such recognition, especially as its outward sign or prize. But the interests of a class must directly refer to standing and rank to status and security, that is, they are primarily not economic but social.[12]

What Polanyi is saying about class in general is just as true about the professional class or individual professions. We know that those occupations that push for professional recognition are often more concerned about social status than enhanced income. But does it really matter which of the three—financial success, social status, or power—is primary or dominant? All three are so linked in the American culture that any one seldom appears without the other two. If so, it should not matter which of the three the individual professional is pushed or pulled toward, because the dilemma would exist in all cases.

There are three basic reasons why it is important to determine which goal is primary and which ones secondary. The first is explanatory. If the primary goal were social status, it would better explain the intense competitiveness not only among the professions but among the individual members as well. Although financial success and power as perquisites of professional life are unlikely to be equally distributed among the various professions, among significant groups inside each profession, or among individuals, they could be distributed in a more equal way without most people feeling they have significantly failed to achieve their goals.[13]

Social status, however, requires relatively sharp differentiation. Not only individuals, but occupational groups as well, strive for social status. It is common for an occupation to aspire to professional status because this will enhance the respect given its practitioners. Once this threshold is reached, there will be a struggle to enhance the occupation in the professional pecking order, where lawyers and medical doctors enjoy the highest prestige (as well as the highest income). Nurses and accountants are toward the lower end of the prestige scale. One can then engage in that time-honored American pastime of ranking the others on a linear scale. Where do ministers or priests, university professors, investment counsellors, architects, teachers, journalists, urban planners, and so on, fall between the extremes?[14]

A second reason to be concerned with the primacy of goals is its utility in analyzing a problem to be discussed later. Is the dilemma tougher for successful professionals or for marginal ones?[15] If financial success is primary, one would expect the success horn of the dilemma to be strongest for marginal performers. If social status is the dominant concern, it would be greatest at the upper reaches of the professions, where the competition for eminence is most intense.

The third reason relates to the problem of remedy. One would select a certain set of causal explanations, attempts at reeducation, and sanctions if dealing with unacceptable ways of striving for financial success; quite different ones would apply if the primary goal is to attain high social status.

The question of primacy is not merely one of polling many individual professionals about their goals. People can be unaware of the true sources of their drives. Certainly the emphasis in our culture on economic motivation for the actions of producers causes people to explain their choices in terms of profit or income. In the last two decades, there has been an enormous increase in the public acceptance and use of neoconservative economic analysis and terminology. Professionals subjected to that education and terminology would naturally use this terminology to explain their behavior.

THE BOTTOM LINE

The "success" horn of the dilemma is the attitude that has come to be known as "bottom line" thinking. *Bottom line* here refers either to the net worth item on the balance sheet prepared by an accountant or to the total remaining when one makes a cost-benefit analysis, that is, subtracts the costs or expenses of a course of action from the benefits or income. In its worst manifestations, this attitude concentrates on short-term profits and seems to regard any means as legitimate toward this end of increasing profits until one gets caught and punished. As Sissela Bok has observed:

> The very stress on individualism, on competition, on achieving material success which so marks our society also generates intense pressure to cut corners. To win an election, to increase one's income, to outsell competitors—such motives impel many to participate in forms of duplicity they might otherwise resist. The more widespread they judge these practices to be, the stronger will be the pressures to join, even compete in deviousness.[16]

From this perspective, the wrongdoing is often seen not as acting improperly, but in getting caught. While one could attribute this "bottom line" attitude to nonprofessional business people,[17] such as entrepreneurs, and contrast it with professional ethical attitudes, it is clear that many business persons work with a strong sense of ethics and many professionals are pure "bottom line" thinkers. "Bottom line" profit-making attitudes so permeate our society that even ethical professionals feel the pressure. In a newspaper article discussing the fact that the average physician in 1989 will earn $152,000, the journalist commented, "In a growing commercialism in medicine, some doctors, other doctors say, think more about the bottom line than they do about their patients. Even the most conscientious doctors are increasingly forced to consider the bottom line."[18] That this applies to all middle-class professionals is the observation of a very perceptive social commentator, Barbara Ehrenreich, who writes:

> Despite repeated announcements of the "end of greed" and increasingly testy calls for "new values," the professional middle class remains on the whole, committed to the pursuit of wealth: syncophantic toward

those who have it, impatient with those who do not, and uncertain about what, if anything, was left behind in the heat of the chase.

Part of the problem is "structural," which is the economist's way of saying that it's no one's fault. Things simply cost more—so much more that we are frequently invited to sympathize with the middle-class breadwinner who can no longer get by on upwards of $100,000 a year.[19]

Questionable professional decisions are often not cynical or evil. Whether a lawsuit should be filed, surgery is necessary, or a particular investment is wise is often a matter of judgment about which reasonable professionals could disagree. We are now, thanks to psychoanalytic discoveries, painfully aware of how easily we can delude ourselves and rationalize self-regarding action. A psychiatrist friend in commenting on this dilemma said, "The Hippocratic Oath and Bar Code demand something that human beings cannot really do . . . give an [unbiased] opinion on a matter you have a strong self interest in."[20] Any ethical expectation that demands conduct impossible or difficult for typical humans may well be in need of reformulation.

NOTES

1. This distinction between the (pure) motive of public service and the (base) motive of extrinsic rewards or success is suggested by Norman Podhoretz, *Making It* (New York: Random House, 1967), 53, where he writes:

> What then are the reasons for the connection between the study of literature and the contempt for success? The noblest of them is undoubtedly that the study of literature encourages a great respect for activity which is its own reward (whereas the ethos of success encourages activity for the sake of extrinsic reward), and a great respect for the thing-in-itself (as opposed to the ethos of success which encourages a nihilistically reductive preoccupation with the "cash value" of all things). To acquire even a small measure of independent critical judgment is to understand that "successful" does not necessarily mean "good" and that "good" does not necessarily mean "successful." From there it is but a short step, the shortest step in the world, to the ardent conclusion

that the two can *never* go together, particularly in America and particularly in the arts.

2. Nonprofessional here does not mean that the business manager may not regard himself or be regarded as a professional, but that he does not share the profession of the members of the association. If he is an accountant or a business manager, he naturally brings the professional goals of that group to the administration of the enterprise. Those goals are often more success- and profit-oriented than the professional ethics of members of the association.

3. This point I owe to Tom Rossi, who told me that keeping clients happy so that you can control them is what "the game is all about" in the large urban law firm. He also added that problems usually arise when the lawyer tries to manipulate clients, rather than serve them.

4. Alfie Kohn, *No Contest: The Case Against Competition* (Boston: Houghton Mifflin, 1986), 4.

5. Some notion of the cost of higher education that is essential to most professionals is shown by the statistics that in 1987–1988, the estimated total cost for an in-state student attending a public college or university was $5,504, compared to $11,568 at an independent college or university. By 1988–1989 these costs had increased to $5,823 at public institutions and $12,525 at independent institutions. This represents in one year a 6 percent increase in the public sector and an 8 percent increase in the independent sector. Forty-three percent of the 1984 graduates of four-year institutions completed college with education debts, of which the average was $5,500. *1989–90 Fact Book on Higher Education*, 187. For the current year the tuition increase moderated slightly, running from 5 to 8 percent. The total cost including tuition, books, and room and board at the ten most expensive private universities was in excess of $22,000 per year. See Michel Marriott, "College Tuition Costs for the Nation Increasing at a Reduced Pace," *New York Times*, Sept. 27, 1990, A13.

6. See Eric Clark, *The Want Makers: Lifting the Lid Off the World Advertising Industry: How They Make You Buy* (London: Hodder & Stoughton, 1988).

7. John Kultgen, *Ethics and Professionalism* (Philadelphia: University of Pennsylvania Press, 1988), 21–22.

8. This simplifies or flattens out a complex set of issues. Whether a service is necessary is different from what the consumer wants. "Want" includes both true needs and false needs. False needs are created in large part by advertising, although advertising may also awaken in the consumer an awareness of a true need. Advertising has certainly contributed to an increased consumption of professional services, an

increase in the "wants." The percentage of that increased consumption that is false or unnecessary is both theoretically and empirically difficult to determine.

9. For the lawyer, this competitive pressure toward financial success in its early stages of professional development of the beginning lawyer is well caught in Scott Turow, *One L* (New York: Putnam, 1977).

10. An example of this sort of pressure placed on highly successful young lawyers is the expectation of major law firms that new associates produce annually 2200 billable hours, which translates into almost 45 hours a week, taking into account vacation time. This means the lawyer must spend more time than that working in the office, since not all the time spent there can be billed. See Elizabeth M. Fowler, "Reducing the Stress on Lawyers," *New York Times*, Jan. 23, 1990, C17.

11. Elizabeth Rosenthal, "Innovations Intensify Glut of Surgeons," *New York Times*, Nov. 7, 1989, B17.

12. Karl Polanyi, *The Great Transformation* (Boston: Beacon Press, 1944, 1957), 153.

13. In the initial stages of redistribution of money or power, those who have been more favored in the original distribution will feel they have lost something to which they were entitled. They will in the short run believe they have failed in their goal not just to have more income or more power than their fellows, but also will feel they are entitled to maintain the gap or disparity.

14. I am not suggesting any such ranking is empirically accurate, because it is highly subjective. Most Americans, however, believe such ranking can be made and it affects the esteem, the rewards, and the power of members of each group.

15. See Chapter 9.

16. Sissela Bok, *Lying: Moral Choice in Public and Private Life* (New York: Vintage Books, 1978), 258.

17. The increasing discussions about corporate social responsibility, about the need for business people to think long term, to act responsibly towards employees and toward communities where they are located, and to avoid polluting the environment may suggest that traditional "bottom line" thinking is losing ground even in the business community.

18. Victor Cohn, "Doctors and Dollars: Is Greed Eroding Care?" *The Topeka Capital-Journal*, Nov. 18, 1989, B1.

19. Barbara Ehrenreich, *Fear of Falling: The Inner Life of the Middle Class* (New York: Pantheon Books, 1989), 244.

20. Letter, dated November 6, 1989, from Stuart W. Twemlow, M.D., to the author.

5

The Dilemma's Context and the Ease of Rationalization

There are three types of unethical behavior in providing professional services. The first is selling unnecessary services. The second is expanding or padding necessary services to increase the charges made to the client. To the extent this exceeds the efficient and competent performance of the needed professional help, such services and their concomitant charges are unnecessary. This could be seen as a subset of the first type of behavior. The third type is the sloppy or incompetent performance of clearly necessary services. Sloppy performance may well be the most serious unethical practice by professionals. It clearly violates the professional's duty to be competent. Most malpractice claims probably arise from this third type.

The setting most clearly showing the conflict between the professional roles of counsellor and of service provider is the provision of unnecessary services. That is the problem context to be clarified in this chapter.

THE ZONES OF DECISION ABOUT NECESSITY

The problem I am interested in is more limited than the whole range of decisions about whether services are necessary. To clarify this, let us assume a continuum along which are ranged all potential decisions about whether a client needs services. Along this continuum, we can identify four zones of decision.

At one end is the first zone—those cases where the procedure is so clearly unnecessary that the attempt to provide services will be met with ridicule or contempt by almost all professionals. This is where the unethical activity is clearest, the provision of unnecessary services usually intentional and indefensible, and the resolution of the dilemma unproblematic.

In the fourth zone at the other end are those cases where all professionals agree the services are necessary; that is, if we stay with my running example of the lawyer, the legal action should be brought.

If it is equally reasonable to defend either position in a controversy, then both lawyers agree that the probabilities of success are grouped around the 50th percentile, but they differ about the direction of result.[1] These are third zone cases.

Between the first zone, defined by the "not being laughed out of court" test, and third zone cases where the court's decision could go either way, there is the second zone—a gray area where the lawyer can perhaps justify providing the services, but prudent and conscientious attorneys would usually advise clients not to expend time and money in an attempt to prevail.[2]

This continuum can be understood better if illustrated with a diagram:

Zone 1	Zone 2	Zone 3	Zone 4
Unnecessary Services	Arguably Unnecessary	Reasonable Disagreement	Clearly Necessary

In the second zone, the gray area, it is hard to define workable guidelines, train professionals to make careful professional and ethical judgments, and enforce good faith on the part of the professional. And yet this is where the ethical dilemma is not only most hidden, but most difficult. The first and fourth zones produce no serious problems of judgment, while the second and third place the professional in a position of exercising judgment. My concern is the second zone, where sound judgment tilts toward regarding the service as unnecessary.

This gray area can be analyzed as one where the institutional structure developed for the professions gives each professional autonomy and discretion. But, as anyone who is familiar with Ronald Dworkin's illuminating discussion[3] of what discretion means will recognize, this does not authorize professionals to make any decision they wish. There are limitations on the way discretion may be exercised. One is the ethical constraint protecting the client's interests, a matter of professional ethics. Another is that the professional must make a reasonable technical judgment, the constraint of professional competence.[4]

Much ethics discussion focuses on zone one—where the services are clearly unnecessary by any criteria. Here, the provision of services is indubitably unethical, and probably actionable as well.[5] These are easy and clear cases. As we move along the continuum into the area of judgment or discretion, ethical issues do not disappear. They merely become more complex and more hidden. The most serious problem may be sloppy practice, but the ethical issue of professional competence in performance applies to the entire continuum of services performed, whatever the degree of necessity. My focus is whether the services are necessary or not. That raises ethical problems about the professional as counsellor.

This analysis is theoretical, rather than empirical. Thus, I make no judgment about how many cases belong in each of the four categories. I assume a substantial percentage fall into the second and third zones, where one cannot easily say either the services are necessary or are blatantly unnecessary. It then becomes a matter of discretion for the professional, a decision calling for not merely technical competence, but ethical judgment.

The definition of professional skills and the process of diagnosis of client problems is controlled by the profession. As stated by Andrew Abbott,

> To investigate the relation of a profession to its work is no simple task. To be sure, the tasks of professions have certain objective qualities that resist professions' efforts to redefine them. But many basic qualities turn out to be subjective qualities assigned by the profession with current jurisdiction. These objective and subjective qualities have a dynamic relation in which neither one predominates. On the one hand, a task's

basis in a technology, organization, natural fact, or even cultural fact provides a strong defining core. On the other, the profession reshapes this core as it pulls the task apart into constituent problems, identifies them for clients, reasons about them, and then generates solutions shaped to client and case. Through this reshaping of objective facts by subjective means there emerges a fully defined task, irreducibly mixing the real and the constructed.[6]

What is necessary is controlled not only by the client's objective needs and subjective wants, but by the profession's conceptual construction in its monopoly of expertise of what clients generally need. Within the constraints of professional concepts and the client's needs and wishes, there is substantial room for an individual practitioner to maneuver in guiding a client toward defining his individual needs in ways that enhance the professional's income.

Much professional activity may be defined intentionally by the organized profession into zones two and three, where there is uncertainty about whether the services are necessary. The conception of professional activity as an area of specialized services where it is always a matter of skilled judgment may be designed to keep other professionals and occupations from encroaching on the professional's monopoly as well as to prevent too strict a regulation or oversight by governmental agencies.[7] There is also difficulty in assessing whether the services have been successful in achieving their anticipated goal.

THE MEANING OF "NECESSARY"

One could describe the problem as one of defining or determining what is necessary. Necessity is not only a technical question, but depends on factors that vary from client to client. When a client consults a lawyer about whether to sue someone, the values could be whether the client is risk-averse or risk-preferring, is interested in harmonious relations with others or is confrontational, is interested in cost-efficient resolutions or has nonmaterial goals in mind. The lawyer's values might vary on these dimensions.

If we think about a patient consulting a physician for treatment, the different value positions could include whether he has a high or low threshold of pain, whether he is adverse to or prefers taking medication, and whether he is cost conscious or willing to invest almost any amount in the improvement of his health, among other factors.

If professionals and their clients share the same values, there should be little difficulty in reaching a mutually satisfactory decision. The ethical requirement that the professional must have the best interests of the client in mind demands that the client's values and wishes be factored into the decision.

One attitude widespread today about how we ought to define necessity, want, or need, is to consider this a matter that is completely the choice of a consumer entering the market. What constitutes a necessity, a luxury, or a want is said to be highly subjective and in a free market economy should be the autonomous choice of the consumer. This attitude neatly solves the problem of what is necessary for the client. Whatever he wants and is willing to pay for is a necessary service.

There are two problems with this approach to defining necessity. A customer who is autonomously deciding about his wants and necessities must have accurate information not only about what is available in the market but also about the utility of the services. He goes to the professional to get that information. If the professional intentionally or inadvertently misleads the customer, we are not justified in treating the decision based on that information as a choice about what is necessary.

The second difficulty with treating the client's expression of his wishes as a satisfactory index to the necessity of services is how adept we have become in manipulating choices. The function of advertising and consumer education has often been analyzed as creating wants, turning false needs into perceived true needs, and moving many goods and services that were earlier perceived as luxury or unnecessary items into the realm of necessities. Services offered by professionals cover the range from essential to desirable to luxury to harmful. The professional, in conjunction with the client, must make a determination about where the service inquired about falls on this continuum. Since it is a judgment that varies with context and with client, it must be an individual decision, partly technical and partly personal. The ethical requirement is that the professional help the client make a decision appropriate for the client.

THE COMPLEXITIES IN THE ZONE OF DECISION

The zones of the continuum we are most concerned with are those areas where professionals would differ in their judgment and advice. The lower the percentage of professionals who would recommend that services are necessary compared to those advising against the services, the closer we come to the zone where the services are clearly unnecessary. A complicating problem, however, is to identify just what it is that the professionals are disagreeing about.

First, there is the question of goal or purpose. Just what is it that the client wants or needs. In theory, that decision belongs exclusively to the client.

Next, there is an instrumental or strategic decision about ways or means of achieving the goal. This would appear to be the province of the professional, since it raises questions of technique and expertise. If we see the problem as primarily an economic issue, and it is certainly at least that, then the obligation of the professional is to select and use the most efficient means of achieving the goal. One possible professional decision could be that there is not any technical means by which the goal could be at least reached within the financial capabilities of the client. Another possible professional decision could, and in appropriate cases should, be that there is not an ethical (or honest) method available to achieve the client's goal.

Actually, these two spheres of decision, the client's as to goal and the professional's as to means, are interrelated. The professional is the one knowledgeable about the costs of various options, not only the financial costs, but also the likely side effects or undesirable consequences of each choice. Clearly, the client's choice of goal has to take into account the strategic or instrumental problems, costs, and consequences.

The professional who intends to provide unnecessary services can do so by recommending the costliest or most complex strategies, as long as these are within the financial capabilities of the client. Or she could, by underemphasizing or not mentioning cheaper, perhaps less safe, ways to achieve the goal, force the client's choice toward the most expensive option.

There is another choice-influencing activity engaged in by professionals that raises serious ethical problems. The professional may at the time of initial choice or commitment underestimate the cost of the strategy or the side effects so that the client at the point of deciding not only on goals, but on the use of the professional's service, believes that the services are not only desirable, but affordable. After services are begun and the client is locked in, other more expensive services may be needed.[8] This possibility emphasizes how important ethical and good faith judgments by the counsellor are at the time the relationship is begun.

THE EASE OF RATIONALIZING DECISIONS
IN THE ZONE OF DISCRETION

Rationalization carries the notion of a justification that is neither an honest nor an adequate explanation, or one that would not be persuasive to an objective person knowing all the facts. Rationalization will be used from two perspectives. One is psychological and involves the actor, in this case the professional, who fools herself about the reasons for action. When our self-interest is involved, we believe justifications for acting in a way that achieves our self-interest, even though those reasons would be unpersuasive to us if our self-interest were not involved. This is a major reason that so many ethics codes prohibit situations in which there is a conflict of interest, when one of the interests is that of the actor. It is easy when making tough choices involving many factors and nice questions of judgment to shade decisions based on what self-interest would dictate and not even be aware you are doing it.

Of course, decisions must also be explained or justified to the client and to the public. The explanations used here can also be rationalizations. If the professional has fooled herself, it is then easy to deceive the client or mislead the public, when some question is raised about the necessity of a particular service. If the professional has not deceived herself and intentionally provides the service knowing it was unnecessary, it is still easy to claim—

because we are in an area of professional autonomy and discretion—that the services were necessary or that the professional honesty believed they were necessary. From this, it is an easy step to argue that the ethical duties of protecting the client's interests have been complied with.

Rationalizations may be made not only by individual practitioners, but also by the profession as an entity to the public. Much public relations activity takes on this quality. An ethical code, to the extent that it is intended to be a representation that the profession is ethical rather than a guideline to the professional on how to act, could also be described as a rationalization, if known to be descriptively untrue.

CONCLUSION

The problems of the context are not only the professional's dilemma of choosing between the welfare of the client and her self-interest, but also the difficult value issues implicit in defining what is necessary, and the complex technical issues of judgment about what services will best satisfy the client's needs and what the chances of success are. These complexities make it easy for an unscrupulous professional to mask her choices and for the insensitive professional to push the problems out of her consciousness.

To improve ethical conduct in this area requires either a structure that eliminates the conflict of interest or an education in which professionals learn to be sufficiently self-aware that they recognize when they are tempted to rationalize. They must become committed to the proposition that every decision they make must be justified or at least justifiable. Rationalization is not enough.

NOTES

1. If the lawyers agree that the probabilities of success are very high and they agree on the direction of result, there should not be litigation because the attorney on the losing side should not contest it. See the discussion by Karl Llewellyn in *The Common Law Tradition: Deciding Appeals* (Boston: Little Brown & Co., 1960), 24–25, 219–22.

2. In *Crisci v. Security Insurance Co.*, 66 Cal.2d 425, 426 P.2d 173 (1967), the Supreme Court of California in an analogous situation suggested a possible test that would ask if the lawyer herself were the party bringing the action, would she sue. If she would not, then it is clearly not in the interest of her client to do so.

3. See Ronald Dworkin, *Taking Rights Seriously* (Cambridge, Mass.: Harvard University Press, 1978), 31–34.

4. One could also include in this analysis the problem where services are necessary, but performed incompetently. The incompetent or sloppy performance of necessary services raises ethical issues as well as problems of technique, because a professional is obligated to perform services competently or send the client to seek services elsewhere.

5. See Chapter 9.

6. Andrew Abbott, *The System of Professionals: An Essay on the Division of Expert Labor* (Chicago: University of Chicago Press, 1988), 57.

7. See Ibid, 46, where the author says:

> Another variable affecting vulnerability [of professional jurisdiction] is the measurability of the results. As results become less and less measurable, there is less and less need to prefer one treatment to another, and thus a weaker professional hold on the problem area. Since the results of psychotherapy are famously difficult to measure, psychotherapeutic schools have become interchangeable and the problems they treat have become an interprofessional battleground. On the other hand, results that are too easily measurable lead to easy evaluation from outside the profession and consequent loss of control. They may also make it easier for competitors to demonstrate treatment superiority if they have it.

8. This is a strategy we have come to expect as almost standard with defense contractors, but it is not unknown for any contractor who must engage in competitive bidding. Of course, the professionals who are on the staff of these contractors, such as accountants, engineers, architects, and business executives, are faced with the same ethical dilemmas discussed in this book. Those who make management decisions are prescribing unnecessary services and acting unethically. Subordinates are faced with the whistle-blower's dilemma. See Chapter 7.

6

The Cost of Unnecessary Services

In the contemporary western world, a common way of analyzing the ethics or value choices involved on any issue is utilitarianism.[1] John Rawls' formulation of this position is: "The basic idea is that society is rightly ordered, and therefore just, when the major institutions are arranged so as to achieve the greatest net balance of satisfaction summed over all the individuals belonging to it."[2] Stated in a form more useful to our purpose, utilitarianism is often collapsed into a cost-benefit analysis, that is, those acts that produce more costs than benefits are unethical (and wasteful). Conversely, actions that are more beneficial than their costs are approved and ethical.[3]

In the discussion in Chapter 3, I preferred to ground the ethical obligation to serve the client's interest in the relationship of trust, in the requirements of competence, and in the grant of professional autonomy. A utilitarian analysis supplements this by showing that the costs of providing excessive or unnecessary services so greatly outweigh the benefits that such services are disutilitarian, and therefore improper. Cost-benefit analysis clearly shows why there is increasing social disapproval of much professional activity. This dissatisfaction is caused in large part by the high cost of professional services, even where services are clearly essential. The best example is the contemporary uproar over the cost of health care. Justifiable and efficient services are already too expensive for many patients. If such costs are inflated by the provision of unnecessary services, it makes the public criticism more powerful.

There are two related but separate perspectives on the problem of excessive cost. One is societal. Is too large a percentage of national income being diverted away from other equally important uses? The second perspective is that of the individual consumer. For him, it is a question of the competing priorities of various potential expenditures in his budget, where there is a finite amount of disposable income. Often a particular professional service, however essential, just cannot be afforded.

THE VARIOUS COSTS ARISING FROM UNNECESSARY SERVICES

Some costs of unnecessary professional services are intangible. There is the expectation that the services will produce some benefit or advantage. If the client learns that those anticipated gains are not achieved, there is disappointment and often anger.

There are intangible costs to the professional as well. Each professional, while making an ongoing series of choices in dilemma situations, is engaged in creating her own moral and personal character as well as her reputation, whether she recognizes that or not. To the extent that her choices in the dilemmas she faces are honest, competent, and loyal, she develops that kind of character. If her choices are shaded toward taking financial advantage, cutting corners, and manipulating clients and others, she becomes, over time, avaricious, untrustworthy, aggressive, and manipulative. The cost of pursuing financial and social success at any price is loss of decency and reputation.

There are also important intangible social costs. Since the professional asks for trust from clients and the public, any abuse of that trust decreases the level of trust in society. In our contemporary competitive world, it may be naive to trust other persons totally, even those most entitled to trust, such as family, friends, and ministers. However, this is not a matter of reciprocity or symmetry. If a trustworthy social environment is desirable, all decent people, including professionals, are obligated to be trustworthy. If professionals are not to be trusted, this sharply diminishes the amount of trust in our world, a commodity that may already belong on the endangered species list.

Other adverse consequences may be tangible, but hard to quantify. In the case of medical or psychological services, there may be damage to body or psyche. For clients of those professionals, such as lawyers, stockbrokers, or financial consultants, who give advice about the rights of property or its management, there may be quantifiable financial loss to the client's property or estate.

The detriment I want to focus on in this chapter is the financial cost of the services themselves. To the individual client, the professional's fee takes more of his income or assets to achieve the goals for which the services were sought than would have been spent if no unnecessary services were sold to him. For society, the cost is allocating an unnecessarily large portion of national income to this sphere of professional activity and as a consequence diminishing the amount available for use in other areas. These represent opportunity costs—the expenditure of money on such services reduces the option to do other things.

Robert Heilbroner has argued that competition in a capitalist free market economy is not for market share, but for a share of capital:

This continuous dissolution and recapture [of capital] is the essence of the process of competition, which can be seen as an element in the working of the system that directly stems from the nature of capital itself. Competition does not simply mean the vying of vendors who sell similar products in a market, which is the way contemporary economics perceives it, but the inescapable exposure of each capitalist to the efforts of others to gain as much as possible of the public's purchasing power.[4]

Independent autonomous professionals can be analyzed as capitalists and entrepreneurs. Their capital is their abstract knowledge, expertise, and skills.[5] Consistent with Heilbroner's analysis, they use these assets in a competition for shares of the public's purchasing power, the national income.

A very successful group has been the medical profession (or, more broadly, health-care professions), whose share of the gross national income exceeds 11 percent and is rising at a rate exceeding inflation. Lawyers may have done nearly as well, but have managed to keep a substantial part of their share hidden, much of it in governmental budget items such as the costs for court systems and for governmental attorneys' offices. Insurance companies and their agents,[6] as well as stockbrokers, have been extremely successful in garnering large and increasing shares of national income.

The educational enterprise and its professionals, the teachers, have had varied success. The public schools have serious problems in maintaining their share or keeping up with inflation. Higher education, particularly respected private universities, have been successful in increasing their income in excess of the inflation rate.

Of course, the share of gross national product that goes to each profession is not lost to the rest of the economy. It is spent by the members of the professions for personal and business needs. Professions in general belong to the service sector of our economy, and are not particularly good at capital accumulation beyond the equipment they need to practice their profession. Still, members of those professions that can obtain a large share of the gross national product live better and have more power and respect. The major difficulty is that the purchasing power of most clients is limited, and professions that overprice their services or provide unnecessary services create budgetary strains and dislocations for those clients.

It is enlightening to note the high correlation between those professions that have been most successful in competing for large shares of national income and those professions that enjoy the greatest autonomy and the highest prestige. The largely unregulated autonomy afforded the higher status professions, or at least the elite members of such professions, permits them to exercise their judgment in ways that expand the amount and type of services performed. The status of these respected professionals also allows them to charge high fees for services.

Without exploring the complicated and tangled questions about whether the distribution of national income or of any individual's income among the professions is fair or wise,[7] and thus whether the share of income and prestige of any one profession is justified in comparison with other professions, it is clear that whatever share goes for unnecessary services is being spent inefficiently and wastefully. That alone would be enough to justify an ethical prohibition against unnecessary services.

THE FUNDING OF PROFESSIONAL COSTS

The problem of how professional services will be funded or paid for is an increasingly difficult one for the members of any profession, certainly for their clients, and for the society. There is the traditional method of payment, that is, the client pays for services out of his own pocket. This is the model used by orthodox microeconomic analysis. Unfortunately, if they had to pay the cost of the services in advance or had to finance it through traditional borrowing mechanisms, a substantial portion of our population would be priced out of the market for professional services. This financing problem is exacerbated by the fact that many professional services, such as the medical emergency or the unexpected lawsuit, are fortuitous and may carry very high price tags. Many potential outlays for professional services can be anticipated, such as the need for medical care or tuition for private schooling. The cost for these "necessities," however, is often so large that it is difficult for an individual to finance them. A family must enjoy a very large income much above the national average to be able to pay with little strain for legal expenses, medical expenses, an adequate insurance program, and the cost of educating their children. These expenses almost invariably enjoy lower priorities than absolutely essential expenditures such as housing, food, clothing, and transportation.

An alternative method of financing professional services is by commission, a percentage of the value of the services performed, which is included in the purchase price. This is a common way to compensate insurance salesmen, stockbrokers, and financial advisors, as well as lawyers for plaintiffs through the use of the contingency fee. One disadvantage with the commission is that it is a direct financial incentive for providing more expensive and often unnecessary services.

Much professional service is now funded by insurance programs, either governmental or private. The insurance mechanism has two advantages. If the circumstances where the services are needed are usually fortuitous, the costs may be spread across the entire pool of persons who might need the services, but cannot be sure whether they will be the ones suffering the loss. If the services can be anticipated, but are very costly, insurance programs provide a kind of budgeting and savings program that works well within certain limits.[8] Both advantages are combined in many insurance programs, such as health insurance.

The reserves created by governmental insurance programs are paid for by taxpayers, either all taxpayers as in social security, or designated groups as in the recently eliminated catastrophic health care program for the elderly. Since not all contributors will receive a median or greater share of the collected reserves, many will have a great incentive to try to keep the costs and the size of the reserves down, or to escape from the pool, if at all possible. This is the operation of what insurance experts call the principle of adverse selection.[9] Clients purchasing private insurance contribute premiums to insurance companies who manage the reserve funds that will be used to pay claims. Those insureds contributing to such reserves who anticipate receiving a median or smaller share of the reserves have an economic incentive to hold costs down, or perhaps to go uninsured.

THE STANDARDS FOR JUSTIFYING
PROFESSIONAL SERVICES

The proper allocation of income to services is increasingly a matter of concern to funding and financing agencies, both governmental departments and insurance companies, that collect, manage, and disburse funds. Their concern is essentially "bottom line" accounting, and their concern is much more a matter of keeping costs in line than in making sound professional judgments about what procedures are used. The funding or insuring agencies may be interested in eliminating waste. They are more likely to be interested in eliminating expensive, risky, or experimental procedures. To the extent that insurers can define what procedures are acceptable as qualifying for compensation, they take the choice or discretion for that decision out of the hands of the client and the professional.

Third party payers not only exercise control over what procedures will be used by professionals, but may also deny the availability of affordable services to groups or classes of clients. Health insurers have recently begun denying coverage or writing insurance for groups that in their view may be susceptible to AIDS, for certain high-risk occupations such as miners, loggers, farmers, pest control service employees, and pilots, and for all employees of small businesses, who are seen to have higher claims than average.[10] There is a limit to the extent to which professionals, even those genuinely committed to public service, can be altruistic or perform charity work. If funding agencies will not cover certain groups, they are excluded from professional care.

The analysis of the primary dilemma to this point has assumed that the only parties interested in the decision are the professional and the client. These two should define the goals to be sought and the appropriate procedures. The cost of the services should then be a function of those decisions. Funding problems, however, introduce a third party—a governmental agency or an insurance company. These payers do not have a direct interest in the welfare, needs, interests, or goals of individual clients, nor do they have much interest in improving the knowledge or skills of the profession—the profession's base of expertise. The interest of third party payers is solely financial—to minimize cost. One would like to think their approach would be to eliminate wasteful and unnecessary services. In fact, it is as likely to be to eliminate essential services to groups that are politically or financially insignificant or to eliminate risky or experimental procedures, which increase current cost, even though they may have a long-term value in improving the knowledge and skills base of the professions.

SUMMARY

It is tempting to view the problem of providing unnecessary services as purely one of economic efficiency. It is costly and inefficient to provide services that do not give benefit to the client. The one most concerned with costs is not the person who needs the service, but the one who provides payment. Increasingly, this is a governmental agency or private insurer. There is a conflict of policies or interests here. The funding agency wants low cost, the professional wants autonomy in making decisions about what services to provide, and the client wants freedom to select whatever service he wants, whether it is efficient or not. The wealthy client has such freedom. The high-prestige professional has such autonomy. Clients who must depend on pooled insurance funds and the lower prestige professionals who service such a clientele do not have nearly as much freedom to choose or as much autonomy in providing service. The tail of cost containment may wag the dog of client freedom and professional choice.

NOTES

1. John Rawls argues that classical utilitarianism and intuitionist conceptions of justice have long dominated our philosophical tradition. See John Rawls, *A Theory of Justice* (Cambridge, Mass.: Harvard University Press, 1971), 41.

2. Ibid, 22.

3. Utilitarianism is actually broader than cost-benefit analysis since maximizing happiness takes into account nonquantifiable and intangible values that cost-benefit perspectives tend to ignore.

4. Robert Heilbroner, *The Nature and Logic of Capitalism* (New York: W. W. Norton, 1985), 57.

5. See Andrew Abbott, *The System of Professions: An Essay on the Division of Expert Labor* (Chicago: University of Chicago Press, 1988), 174:

The "new class" [of professionals] comprises individuals in the peculiar position of possessing small bits of capital—their knowledge—but forced in most cases to work for wages. The knowledge "capital" is actually controlled by, and largely produced by, the organized professional group and its institutions.

6. The insurance industry's share of capital is said to account for 13 percent of America's gross national product. Letter from Robert Hunter, President, National Insurance Consumer Organization, 121 N. Payne Street, Alexandria, VA 22314, received by the Washburn University Law Library on August 31, 1990.

7. This raises a fascinating set of questions, which are unfortunately (or perhaps fortunately for me) far beyond the scope of this book.

8. If the total cost to the pool of insureds becomes burdensome, the premium payers will insist on lower premiums, which leads to efforts to curtail the benefits available.

9. See Robert E. Keeton and Alan I. Widiss, *Insurance Law,* student ed. (St. Paul: West Publishing Co., 1988), 14:

Adverse selection occurs whenever potential insureds are treated alike irrespective of some factor that differentiates them as insurance risks. When an insurer does not distinguish among potential insureds, a disproportionately high percentage of applications for insurance will usually come from the less desirable applicants because they get a better bargain.

10. Milt Freudenheim, "Health Insurers, to Reduce Losses, Blacklist Dozens of Occupations," *New York Times,* Feb. 5, 1990, A1.

7

The Whistle-Blower's Purgatory

This chapter about whistle-blowing is a diversion from the primary dilemma created by the competing drives to protect the welfare of the client and to be a social and financial success. The digression is necessary to give a full picture of the problems this dilemma causes other professionals and society. This requires discussing the more complex ethical choices facing the whistle-blower. *Whistle-blower* is a popular term for a member of a team or group, often a subordinate, who notices that a superior or another member of the professional team, or the team as a whole, is acting illegally or unethically, and who notifies the authorities or someone else of his observation, thus "blowing the whistle" on the activity. Her dilemma is whether she should notify the appropriate authorities in the profession, governmental regulators, or perhaps the press, or whether she should remain quiet and acquiesce in the improper activity.

THE PROBLEM OF DETECTING UNETHICAL ACTIVITY

The autonomy given to professionals and their monopoly on expertise make it easier for unethical or illegal activity, including the provision of unnecessary services, to go undiscovered. The client may learn, or more likely suspect, that the services sold him were excessive and make a complaint, but the combination of trust encouraged by the professional and the feeling of inadequacy most clients have about understanding what the professional is doing make it unlikely that the client will discover or report improprieties.

The more likely discoverer of improprieties will be a fellow professional working closely with the acting professional, who has both the opportunity to observe the performance of services and the expertise to judge them. An even more likely observer is a subordinate professional, either a junior to the senior actor, or a member of a supporting profession. A third possible observer is an accountant called in to audit the books of a professional or of a business employing professionals.[1] If the accountant sees something in the documents she is examining that indicates unethical or illegal activity, does she have an obligation to inform? If so, whom? A superior in the organization that hired her, the party who has been injured, or public authorities?

A colleague who is a peer of the actor has a difficult and genuine ethical dilemma to face. The subordinate to the actor has all of the same ethical problems plus substantial social and financial disincentives to informing. The outside auditor has the worry about sacrificing the atmosphere of trust necessary to perform her responsibilities.

A COMPLEX ETHICAL DILEMMA

The subordinates or fellow professionals who are in the best position to observe unethical and illegal activities are those who are members of a team working for a particular client. Examples are a junior associate working with a senior partner in a law firm, a junior accountant on an auditing team, or a surgical nurse or anesthesiologist assisting in an operation.

The Duty of Loyalty

There is a strongly recognized duty of loyalty to the group, an ethical imperative we all learn very early on the school grounds, or perhaps even earlier in the family. One does not inform on classmates to the teacher or principal. One is not supposed to tattle to parents about the activities of a sibling. This duty of loyalty to significant persons or groups is so strong that many of us regard the most offensive feature of totalitarian systems to be their expectation of and compulsion on citizens to inform on family members, neighbors, and fellow workers.

This obligation of loyalty to the groups one belongs to has great utility and ethical strength. A functioning family or team requires an atmosphere of openness and trust among its members. A team of professionals where members have to be suspicious of each other and guarded about what they say or do in the presence of other team members would be much less effective than a team where there is open discussion in an atmosphere of mutual trust.

That duty of loyalty is, of course, not absolute. There are hardly any adults in this society, and few children, who have not been faced with a situation in which they are torn between loyalty to a friend and a feeling that they should report some activity to a responsible person when the friend is committing a crime or hurting third persons.

The Duty to Inform

Just as we have a strong cultural norm against the informer, we have an equally strong contempt for the person who watches people being hurt and does not want to get involved—who just stands on the sidelines doing nothing. We admire the good samaritan and condemn the pharisee who walked by. We are horrified by the bystanders who watch a woman being raped or killed and who do nothing. We have nothing but disgust for the mother who watches the father commit incest with a daughter and who seems to condone it. There is clearly a duty to inform to protect third parties from further injury, especially when third parties are unable to protect themselves because of lack of knowledge, strength, or social position. This becomes more difficult when the actor is a person close to the informer, and one for whom the informer feels or owes loyalty. The choice between the duty of loyalty to a friend and the duty to protect people being injured by that friend may well be the most difficult ethical conflict faced by people at all levels of sophistication in society. And unlike the primary dilemma that is the main subject of this book, the dilemma is a clear ethical one, because the duty of loyalty and the duty to protect persons being injured are both clear ethical obligations.

This obligation to inform authorities about unprofessional conduct of colleagues or other members of the same profession has been clearly articulated in some codes. This is a clear duty of lawyers. Disciplinary Rule 1-103(A) of the American Bar Association's Model Code of Professional Responsibility provides:

A lawyer possessing unprivileged knowledge of a violation of DR 1-102 [specifying misconduct] shall report such knowledge to a tribunal or other authority empowered to investigate or act upon such violation.

This has been reiterated and strengthened by Model Rule 8.3 (a), which provides:

A lawyer having knowledge that another lawyer has committed a violation of the rules of professional conduct that raises a substantial question as to that lawyer's honesty, trustworthiness or fitness as a lawyer in other respects, shall inform the appropriate professional authority.[2]

The American Medical Association's Principles of Medical Ethics also specify such a duty:

9.04   DISCIPLINE AND MEDICINE.
A physician should expose, without fear or favor, incompetent or corrupt, dishonest or unethical conduct on the part of members of the profession. Questions of such conduct should be considered, first, before proper medical tribunals in executive sessions or by special or duly appointed committees on ethical relations, provided such a course is possible and provided also, that the law is not hampered thereby. If doubt should arise as to the legality of the physician's conduct, the situation under investigation may be placed before officers of the law, and the physician-investigators may take the necessary steps to enlist the interest of the proper authority.[3]

The Role Relationships

The peer professional who observes a colleague in unprofessional conduct has a series of role relations, which can conflict:

1. Professional to professional: There is a duty of loyalty to the colleague.
2. Professional to the client who is being injured: If the observing professional is a member of a team or a firm that has been hired by the client, even though she is not working directly for the client, there is a duty owed to see that the group or firm's client is not injured.
3. Professional to the public: Even if the observing professional owes no direct duty to the client being injured, that client is a member of the public and professionals owe duties to citizens who are being injured by members of their profession that is as strong or stronger than the duties one citizen owes another.
4. Professional to the profession as an entity: A professional owes a duty to the profession to support and improve it. That duty may cut both ways in this difficult dilemma. If the dereliction becomes public, it will damage the public's opinion of the profession as a whole. On the other hand, unethical professional conduct should not be condoned. Furthermore, unethical practices feed public condemnation of the profession and need to be rooted out wherever possible.
   If the observer of unethical or illegal conduct is a subordinate professional, there is an additional role conflict.
5. Professional to employer: Employers expect and demand loyalty from their employees, which includes deference, if not obedience, to the policy and professional decisions made by employers. For those professional decisions in zones two and three where competent professionals may differ,[4] the subordinate professional may have an easier ethical responsibility, because she could rely on the decision being the responsibility of the employer.[5] When, however, it becomes clear that the employer is acting improperly, the dilemma of the subordinate becomes very hard indeed.

THE CONSEQUENCES OF WHISTLE-BLOWING

If a subordinate or fellow professional blows the whistle on the improper activity of a superior or coprofessional, there are three possible adverse consequences to the informer that can be anticipated much of the time.[6] The first is that the subordinate may lose her job. Variants are that she will not be promoted or she may be transferred to insignificant activity in such a peripheral area that she will never again have a chance to observe superiors in any activity of importance. This would restrict any further opportunity for career advancement. A second consequence is professional ostracism or blacklisting. The third consequence and one most sure to occur is the loss of trust by fellow professionals, even those of such good faith or competence that they ought not fear any observation of their activities. This is a subtle but real problem.

Fellow professionals are never sure about the motivation of a whistle-blower. Was the reason for reporting to carry out the ethical obligation to protect the client, the public, or the profession? Or was it envy about a more successful and prestigious colleague? Or could it have been anger at some real or supposed slight or insult? Since charges of unprofessional conduct are easy to make and hard to disprove, fellow professionals, even of unimpeachable background and character, would naturally shy away from colleagues who have a propensity to make such charges, as established by the fact that they have already done so.

THE PROBLEM OF PROTECTION AND SUPPORT

The socially conditioned feeling of loyalty to fellow professionals is so strong that the ethical duty to report unprofessional conduct is seldom compelling enough to overcome such reluctance. In the area of criminal enforcement, it has been common to offer financial rewards or tolerance of wrongdoing by the informant as strong incentives to reporting improprieties, but such a reward structure would be unseemly to motivate professionals to inform on other professionals. What is needed is support and recognition for the whistle-blowing professional. Ostracism after blowing the whistle is a disincentive to all other professionals to make such reports.

The whistle-blower must be protected from retaliation by either the superior who committed the improprieties or by colleagues. It is possible to prevent such retaliation as firing, demoting or transferring a whistle-blower.[7] It is more difficult, if not impossible, to guarantee there will be no opportunity costs, that is, failure to promote her or give her higher remuneration, nor can there be a guarantee there will be no loss of trust by fellow workers. The negative intangible consequences of loss of opportunity or of trust is usually so strong, particularly against junior or subordinate professionals dependent upon approval and support by their seniors, that the likelihood they will report infractions by those superiors approaches zero.

If the profession seriously wants to impose a duty of reporting improper professional activity and to develop a reporting mechanism that works, it must go beyond the negative one of protecting whistle-blowers against retaliation to a positive one of support and appreciation, while at the same time avoiding the appearance of "buying" informers.

One possible solution is to provide a mechanism of reporting to an agency or official outside the professional bureaucracy or work group in which the subordinate is functioning. The identity of the informer must be kept in confidence until an investigation has been made to determine whether the charges appear to be true. The problem is that in a proceeding to take some action against the accused professional, such as revoking a license or issuing a reprimand, due process notions will often require that the informant be identified and that the accused have an opportunity to confront her in public. At that point, the repercussions against the whistle-blower will still occur. The fear of this ultimately happening is what sometimes drives subordinates outside the approved methods of reporting unethical behavior and into the hands of the media. Reporters have a much better record for protecting the confidentiality of their sources than any other professional group.[8]

NURSING AS AN EXAMPLE

There is probably no profession that must face the complex ethical issues of whistle-blowing more than nurses. They regularly work as team members with one of the most prestigious of all professions, physicians. They have the expertise both from education and experience to understand what the doctor is doing and why.[9] Since nurses are subordinate and helping professionals to the doctor, they need to have sufficient understanding to carry out his orders according to their spirit, rather than just mechanically. Furthermore, nurses have more personal contact with patients and owe stronger duties both personally and professionally to protect the patient's welfare. At the same time, the nurse owes great loyalty and respect to the professional judgments of the doctor. If the nurse sees the doctor perform unnecessary, excessive, or incompetent services, she is torn between loyalty to the medical/health care team members, both her own and the doctor's, and at the same time, a strong duty to act for the welfare of the patient.

This has led the nursing profession to deal with the problem in great detail in its code of ethics, which provides:

3   The nurse acts to safeguard the client and the public when health care and safety are affected by the incompetent, unethical, or illegal practice by any person.

3.1 SAFEGUARDING THE HEALTH AND SAFETY OF THE CLIENT

The nurse's primary commitment is to the health, welfare, and safety of the client. As an advocate for the client, the nurse must be alert to and take appropriate action regarding any instances of incompetent, unethical, or illegal practice by any member of the health care team or the health care system, or any action on the part of others that places the rights or best interests of the client in jeopardy. To function effectively in this role, nurses must be aware of the employing institution's policies and procedures, nursing standards of practice, the Code for Nurses, and laws governing nursing and health care practice with regard to incompetent, unethical, or illegal practice.

3.2 ACTING ON QUESTIONABLE PRACTICE

When the nurse is aware of inappropriate or questionable practice in the provision of health care, concern should be expressed to the person carrying out the questionable practice and attention called to the possible detrimental effect upon the client's welfare. When factors in the health care delivery system threaten the welfare of the client, similar action should be directed to the responsible administrative person. If indicated, the practice should then be reported to the appropriate authority within the institution, agency, or larger system.

There should be an established process for the reporting and handling of the incompetent, unethical, or illegal practice within the employment setting so that such reporting can go through official channels without causing fear of reprisal. The nurse should be knowledgeable about the process and be prepared to use it if necessary. When questions are raised about the practices of individual practitioners or of health care systems, written documentation of observed practices or behaviors must be available to the appropriate authorities. State nurses associations should be prepared to provide assistance and support in the development and evaluation of such processes and in reporting procedures.[10]

These provisions are admirable for the skillful way they try to deal with all the issues raised by the whistle-blower situation. Nurses clearly have an explicit duty to watch the performances of other members of the health care team they are working with, and to protect the client who might be injured by improper practices. To cover the situation where the proposed action is merely negligent or careless, the nurse, like any good team player, should call it to the attention of the professional acting improperly so it can be corrected immediately without doing damage either to the patient or to the professional involved.

If that is not sufficient, the nurse is expected to report the improper activity to the appropriate agency or authority for remedial action. While it is possible for anyone working in the health care facility, including laboratory technicians, medical specialists, orderlies, and so forth, to take action adverse to the client's welfare, the person most dangerous and worrisome to nurses is the physician, who is their superior and enjoys more prestige and authority. There is almost a pleading tone in paragraph 3.2 of the nurses' code, asking the health care institutions, primarily hospitals, to set up practices and procedures that permit nurses to make reports and be protected against reprisal. It is clear that fear of reprisal from physicians is present and realistic for nurses. Given that fact, one would expect nurses in most instances, except for the most egregious activity, to overlook improprieties and not take any action.

The one channel not mentioned in the code and probably considered inappropriate, but one utilized by whistle-blowers who are fearful of reprisal, is the press. Reporters will not be intimidated by threats of professional reprisal, and they are generally very good about protecting the anonymity of their sources. From a profession's perspective, this is the least desirable way of dealing with unethical practice, except perhaps for legal action. It is completely outside their control and, given the notoriety the press can bring to improper actions, it has a damaging effect on the reputation of the entire profession. Genuinely open and fair procedures within the profession would be preferable for dealing with this problem. The profession, however, must guarantee real access to all complainants, must provide a prompt investigation and resolution machinery, and must protect the informer against illegitimate reprisals.

SUMMARY

The context at the heart of this book, where the professional is faced with a choice of providing unnecessary and excessive services and thereby increasing her compensation or of protecting the interest of the client, is one the professional prefers to keep hidden. It can be most easily detected by colleagues or by subordinate professionals who are cooperating with the acting professional or can at least observe her performance. This places an often excruciating ethical dilemma on the observers. Should they be bound by their loyalty to the fellow professional and not report the violation, or does their duty, often direct, to protect the welfare of the client or public require them to report. If they choose to report the improper activity, they are likely to suffer reprisals ranging from blacklisting or loss of employment to loss of trust from other professionals, a kind of professional purgatory. Still, the autonomy given to professionals cannot be expanded to the point of not being subject to supervision or accountability. If the professions do not provide procedures and support for reports and investigations, the whistle-blowers, when pushed by frustration caused by their difficult ethical dilemma, are likely to resort to the media or to lawsuits, a decision to be feared and avoided by those professions that want to honestly police their own members. For those professions that are not sincere in trying to police their members, it is a result they deserve.

NOTES

1. See Alison Leigh Cowan, "S. & L. Backlash Against Accountants," *New York Times*, July 31, 1990, C1:

> In an effort to prevent another costly bailout like the one mounted on behalf of the savings and loan industry, Federal legislators are drafting a measure that would require independent auditors to alert regulators to any obvious illegal activities they discover in their audits. Now, if accountants happen upon illegal acts, they must notify upper management and drop the account if the client refuses to correct the problem.

Predictably, accountants were not at all happy about having this duty thrust upon them by the proposed legislation.

2. American Bar Association, *Model Rules of Professional Conduct*, 1983, 1987, Rule 8.3(a).

3. Rena A. Gorlin, ed., *Codes of Professional Responsibility* (Washington, D. C.: Bureau of National Affairs, 1986), 124.

4. See discussion of the four zones of decisions in the problem context discussed in Chapter 5.

5. There has been an explicit rule adopted by the American Bar Association's Model Rules of Professional Conduct to deal with this:

RULE 5.2   RESPONSIBILITIES OF A SUBORDINATE LAWYER

(a) A lawyer is bound by the rules of professional conduct notwithstanding that the lawyer acted at the direction of another person.

(b) A subordinate lawyer does not violate the rules of professional conduct if that lawyer acts in accordance with the supervisory lawyer's reasonable resolution of an arguable question of professional duty.

Thomas D. Morgan and Ronald D. Rotunda, eds., *1989 Selected Standards on Professional Responsibility* (Westbury, N.Y.: Foundation Press, 1989), 158.

6. It is often the fear of employer retaliation that keeps subordinate employees in line, even when the reality would likely be less terrifying if the employee tested it. This is caught nicely by Norman Podhoretz,

when he describes an editor under whom he was working, whose dominant concern was to anticipate what his immediate superior would want or not want. See Norman Podhoretz, *Making It* (New York: Random House, 1967), 222.

7. An example is 10 U.S.C.A. §1034(b), which provides:

Prohibition of retaliatory personnel actions.—
No person may take (or threaten to take) an unfavorable personnel action, as a reprisal against a member of the armed forces for making or preparing a communication to a Member of Congress or an Inspector General that under subsection (a) may not be restricted. Any action prohibited by the preceding sentence (including the threat to take any action and the withholding or threat to withhold any favorable action) shall be considered for the purposes of this section to be a personnel action prohibited by this section.

8. The lawyer could probably make an equal claim to protecting confidentiality, but actually the lawyer is torn between two duties. She has a strong obligation to protect the confidence of a client. At the same time, any lawyer has a strong professional commitment to maintaining the integrity of fair procedures for determining fault or guilt. These procedures require public confrontation of the accused and accuser and militate against maintaining the anonymity of an accuser.

9. See "Many Nurses Say 30% of Operations Not Needed," *New York Times*, Feb. 19, 1981, C5. Surgical nurses may be in an excellent position to observe whether a surgeon is performing an unnecessary operation. They are much more willing to answer a news survey anonymously than to go through formal complaint procedures. When this note was read in manuscript form by a nurse and by a medical doctor, the nurse agreed that her profession was in a good position to make such observations, whereas the doctor strenuously disagreed on the ground that nurses are trained technically, but not as diagnosticians.

10. Gorlin, ed., *Codes of Professional Responsibility*, 155.

8

Redefining the Ethical Obligation

One way to ease the dilemma is to redefine the ethical obligation to bring it more in line with choices actually made.[1] While theoretically available, this option may be neither practical nor desirable. Considering its ramifications, however, helps illuminate the ethical problem for the professional, for the profession, and for professional educators.

THE NECESSARY CONDITIONS FOR CHANGE

The problem of redefinition might not appear impossible or even difficult, because ethical codes can be rewritten. The codes, however, memorialize or articulate professional ethics, rather than create them. I argued in Chapter 3 that the duty to refrain from advising or performing unnecessary services arose from the trust placed in the professional, from the autonomy granted to professionals by society, and from the requirements of professional competence. Real and effective redefinition of this ethical obligation could be accomplished only by altering the conditions that the client is expected to trust the professional and that the professional is expected to perform competently. Merely stating these changes, which are necessary conditions of real, as opposed to merely nominal, reformulation, rebuts from the outset that this is a genuine option.

If one wanted to suggest a reformulation to minimize the gaps between ethical expectation and actual performance, how would it be done? Would we want to formally state that the goal of success is so important that the professional is entitled to perform unnecessary or excessive service as long as the client or nobody else complains? This would, of course, eliminate the dilemma by adopting the most unethical practices as our normative expectation. That constitutes the abandonment of ethics. If we are unwilling to do that, should we seek some middle ground by watering down the expectation and, if so, in what ways?

Instead of trying to restate the obligation in a form that weakens or formally abrogates the ethical obligation, we could just eliminate any references to the duty or obligation. Since we seem to have tacitly agreed not to discuss or highlight this duty to serve clients by only providing necessary services, that might closely reflect the current situation. Professional ethical codes and ethics education often degenerate into discussions of highly specific fact problems and duties, without much emphasis on the more general obligation to serve a client faithfully and competently. The lowering of pressure along the horn of ethical service to the client and others requires more than not mentioning the duty, given the degree to which the professional's obligation is implicitly understood and internalized by many professionals. Minimizing guilt and decreasing ethical pressure toward service require affirmative statements and any affirmative justification for client exploitation is what we ought not to do.

Destroying the relationship of confidence and reliance between clients and professionals is undesirable. No society or economy can function without certain levels of trust. In smaller and older communities, long-term relationships based on personal and family connections between customers and professionals helped assure a high level of responsible advice. A professional who consistently performed below acceptable standards or provided excessive or unnecessary services would soon find that her reputation for such activity was becoming well known and she would start losing clients to competitors. In larger urban communities, these relational inhibitors, including reliable information about reputation, are much weaker or totally absent. In an increasingly complex and alienated society, the normative role of formal ethical codes in reinforcing older notions of reciprocity and trust has become more important.

THE LEVEL AT WHICH CHANGE IS NECESSARY

It is important to distinguish between the formal ethical positions to which formal allegiance is paid and those real rules of conduct governing actual choices made by people, that is, the ethical system that matters to individuals. It is this second level where ethical values actually function. The adverse consequences of unethical action are not only the undesirable social and personal consequences for others or for the acting professional, but the guilt produced inside the professional by the questionable choice. The guilt means that the dilemma has been internalized into the professional's conscience, so any genuine reformulation of the ethical obligations of professionals must reach this level.

The real choice between service and success that bothers professionals in day-to-day situations is determining how much weight ought to be given each aim as balances are drawn in actual contexts of professional judgment. In large urban communities, that balance is being struck differently than it used to be in smaller, tightly knit communities. Since we are concerned with the ethical dimension, it is not so much each individual, discrete choice that is critical. Rather, it is the attitude of professionals and the relative weights they are inclined to give each aim that are significant.

The problem in identifying whether the dilemma exists and what potential choices might be available has been worsened by the increased difficulty of making clear and defensible judgments about whether services are necessary. Not only are the contexts within which a professional acts more complex and the types of services more sophisticated, but there has been a change in attitudes about the nature of professional knowledge. We seem to be less sure that there are correct or true answers to any of the theoretical or practical questions faced by professionals. In

the field with which I am most familiar, attorneys are less willing to make judgments about probabilities of success, so if the
case meets the most minimal threshold of plausability, that is,
the professional will not be laughed out of court, the suit will
frequently be brought and defended. Many lawyers believe, or
at least contend, that one can never predict accurately what a
court will do, and thus the client is entitled to an authoritative
decision about his rights.

The complexity of technical decision makes it easier for the
professional to overlook that there is an ethical dimension at all,
and to the extent it is recognized, to rationalize taking the path
dictated by self-interest.

THE UTILITY OF GUILT

Redefining the ethical obligation to make it conform more to
contemporary practice would have the decided advantage of
eliminating substantial guilt and anxiety in professionals. This
may not be a desirable or achievable goal. "A good part of a
man's ethics consists of the ways in which he copes with his
temptations."[2] The gap between ethics and temptation is buried
deep within the culture and psyche. They cannot be altered just
by an act of will or a rewriting of a formal code.

Although one ought to view the ethical obligation as the epito-
me of internal motivation, it is interesting how much we use
external factors, first as a justification for any particular ethical
expectation, secondly as a way of explicating or applying the
obligation, and finally as a means or strategy to encourage or
compel compliance. A utilitarian analysis forces us explicitly to
look to external factors. Internal motivation is, however, what
causes the actor to comply. That motivation is primarily the result of the individual's conscience and the sense of guilt she
feels when not doing what she "ought" to do. In the twentieth
century, we are a very guilt-ridden people. For the professional
caught in the dilemma between the horn of serving the public and that of striving for financial success and social status
guilt levels are likely to continue to increase, whichever choice
is made. Electing to pursue financial and status goals produces

high levels of guilt, not only because the ethical obligation has been disobeyed, but also due to a strong residue of the puritan attitude that there is something sinful about being covetous of pleasure and display. On the other hand, choosing to devote oneself to the less rewarding activities of professional service leaves high levels of guilt about whether one has been fair to oneself, to one's parents who prepared one for success, and to one's dependents who must also enjoy more modest amounts of material want-satisfaction than their friends.

One of the most important goals of psychological therapy, particularly the pop varieties, is to relieve the person of guilt. Some manifestations of New Age philosophy are intended to persuade Yuppies that it is perfectly all right to pursue financial self-interest.[3]

In any event, we seem to have learned to tolerate or live with high levels of guilt. Is that inevitably a bad thing? To the extent that guilt is the product of conflicts caused by competing sets of goals, both of which cannot be achieved, or else arises from an ambiguous social situation with unclear guidelines about right action, guilt about choices made is unavoidable. The elimination of guilt then becomes an impossible goal. This insight was caught a century ago by Oliver Wendell Holmes, Jr., when he wrote: "The logical method and form flatter that longing for certainty and for repose which is in every human mind. But certainty generally is illusion, and repose is not the destiny of man."[4]

Whether guilt is a good or bad thing depends on the goal it is attached to, on whether it is directed to choices that could have been made another way (that is, the actor can relieve the guilt by acting in the proper way), and on whether the amount of guilt reaches levels that debilitate the professional from acting. In the field of professional ethics, we might attempt to increase the guilt feelings attached to violating the ethical injunction and to minimize those attached to not achieving high levels of financial success and social status.

To the extent that the conscience of the professional and her guilt feelings are sufficiently strong to keep the professional acting in ethical ways, this minimizes the need for external pressure or constraints on professional conduct and thus protects professional autonomy.

THE NEED FOR EXPLICIT AND HIGH ETHICAL EXPECTATIONS

There is a virtue to clear and serious ethical directives. The ethical rules prohibiting unnecessary services are often explicit and always at least implicit in all of the professions. The problem facing the professional, however, is not so much knowing what is ethical, but in applying it in areas of complex and difficult professional judgments. The actual worries of the professional are probably a congeries of decisions in answer to a series of related questions, which include: Did I act ethically? Did I have all the relevant information? Did I get the technical judgments right? Was the service really necessary? Was it what the client genuinely wanted?

The goal should not be reformulation of the ethical directive, but better elaboration of the obligation. What the professional needs is not an easier ethical standard, but much better guidelines and training in how to make these related judgments. This will not minimize the dilemma, because the horn of the dilemma representing success and financial pressure remains very powerful. Better articulated standards, however, would make it more difficult to rationalize or justify questionable activity.

When the focus is on the provision of unnecessary services, there is a temptation to view the dilemma as primarily a problem of cost containment. This has dominated the discussion about ethical problems in the health care system. Redefining the ethical prescription to legitimate current practices would not improve the cost situation, and might actually worsen it. One result might be that clients would be forced into more realism by making them as suspicious or distrustful of their lawyer, their doctor, or their investment counsellor, as they are of their auto mechanic or plumber.

Professional ethics have developed as a consequence of viewing careers like law, medicine, investment counselling, and so on as something other than businesses or mere occupations. If a profession is defined as different from an occupation in large measure because of the existence of special ethical obligations and a commitment to public service and welfare of the clients, but in fact professionals act exactly the same as business people,[5] this raises the basic question of whether the distinction is justified. Critics of the professions claim that professional ethics are a veneer masking a monopoly over an area of expertise in order to exclude competitors. If professionals merely choose a particular occupation as a way of making money, why should we expect them to act differently from entrepreneurs, bankers, auto mechanics, and so forth? If professions are monopolies, should we in evaluating them use the attitude we bring to economic monopolies? Nobody has ever accused a classic monopolist of being interested in the welfare of his customers. Developing ethical norms that start from the proposition that professionals are interested only in enhancing their income appears to have the virtue of being honest, and would permit the society to select one of two correctives. Either customers can be put on notice that they need to protect themselves, or there must be more stringent social regulation. The growing use of malpractice actions may indicate that we are moving toward the second of these alternative consequences.

While realism and honesty are important values for me, I am reluctant to weaken the norm that the professional must further the best interests of the client. Without strong ethical norms, the aspirational or restraining quality of the norm is undermined. Reformulation might be understood as officially legitimating the practice of ruthlessly pursuing the professional's business interests at the expense of the client. Public awareness of a more lax ethical standard would further weaken the public's confidence in the professions, which is already seriously eroded.

If there is to be no reformulation because we are satisfied that formal ethical obligations have been properly defined, the appropriate question is how we can compel or encourage compliance with those guidelines. This is a familiar inquiry to the lawyer, the political regulator, and the social, if not moral, theorist. How do we bring conduct in line with defined norms?

THE HUMAN RIGHT TO MAKE MISTAKES

The heading for this section is a translation from the title of a recent provocative book by a German social theorist, Bernd Guggenberger, entitled *Das Menschenrect auf Irrtum*. The following passage presents his thesis and central concerns:

Once again: To err is human. Not to be allowed to make mistakes is not appropriate to the nature of man. A world that forbids error is an inhumane world. Can there be any doubt that every day we clothe our world with more structures that do not allow error, whether collective or individual? That we prescribe and further develop relationships in life under which we are no longer permitted to make mistakes, whether in crossing the street or taking pills, whether by adopting an energy policy or by irreversible broad-scale urban planning, whether in the cockpit of a jumbo jet or in the control room of an atomic reactor?

Errare humanun est! For too long we have misunderstood this sentence. We are accustomed to interpret it as if it diagnosed a defect. Perhaps we should instead interpret it in the sense of an honor or distinction—as a statement of what actually makes a person human, what distinguishes him in particular from other living beings: Only the human can make mistakes and then learn from them, unless, that is, he creates a world in which errors unavoidably threaten life, if not the entire human race.

When, however, it belongs to the essential nature of man to enrich and broaden himself and his circumstances through the experience of error, then there has to be something like a *human right to make mistakes*, or to state it differently, a duty to create and preserve a mistake-friendly environment. When an important part of the superiority of man consists of an ability to learn from *trial and error*, then it is essential to do everything necessary to retain this type of learning and experience. [My translation.][6]

There is a great danger in stating the ethical expectations for professionals, or for anyone, in a form that treats mistakes as defects and unacceptable under all conditions. There must always be a tension between ordinary levels of conduct and ethical expectations, but the ethics must be based on a realistic understanding of human nature and human potential. It is not merely a question of tolerating mistakes, but rather the celebration of certain kinds of mistakes as a part of our techniques of learning and of making progress. One can separate in theory three kinds of mistakes. The first is that minimum number of mistakes that even the most conscientious and competent professionals will make just because they are human, rather than divine or omnipotent. The second is mistakes that occur in taking reasonable chances or risks that may be necessary and provide the sort of experience from which learning and progress are likely to come. The third type is careless and avoidable mistakes that normal care and competence would have prevented. The way we state our ethical obligations should tolerate the first, encourage the second, and severely discourage the third.

What is important, then, is to recast (not restate) the ethical obligations by importing an understanding that they state goals that should lead the professional to strive to always be better. In other words, there must be tolerance for deviations that arise from ethical activity. There must also be obligation not to hide mistakes, so that the actor and other professionals may learn from them.

THE ZONE FOR AUTONOMY

The appropriate social response to the problem of providing unnecessary services might vary with the zones along the continuum.[7] In that area where no reasonable professional would consider the services necessary, it may be acceptable to use legal sanctions to compel compliance. This zone is where we most likely find intentionally unethical conduct, since competent professionals would realize the services are useless or of only dubious necessity. In the gray area where reasonable professionals would probably advise that the services are not necessary, a competent professional might in good faith do so or might just make a mistake in judgment that should not be characterized as culpable or bad faith. Even the most competent and ethical professionals are human and must be allowed some tolerance for an occasional mistake in judgment.[8] In the zones of professional discretion, compliance has been left to the professional's judgment, and that might well be the wisest social resolution of the dilemma. The appropriate ethical concern, then, would be to educate professionals so they are more aware of ethical guidelines and more explicit in making defensible judgments that do not turn on their self-interest, but rather on the welfare of the client.

THE PROBLEM OF REGULATORY STANDARDS

If we decide this matter cannot be left solely to the professional's conscience, there must be some supervision, whether by the regulatory professional boards, by governmental regulators, or by the courts. The problem is to establish workable standards. Such standards must offer realistic solutions to the problems of applying the norm in the various complex judgmental situations professionals are faced with. It would be undesirable for the standards to be formulated in terms of routinized and cautious practice. Even if the formal standards are more liberal and open-ended, defensive professional practice could well lead to routinized and cautious practices in order to avoid any possible claim of impropriety. The loss of professional innovation and restricting the use of risky procedures where they are appropriate would indeed be costly to our society.

NOTES

1. This is the problem raised by any normative system. If the gap between the norm and typical conduct is too great, the norm will be largely ignored. If the norm merely restates average conduct, there is little need for any normative guideline. Maintaining the appropriate gap or tension so that the guidelines can restrain and change conduct without being ignored is a difficult problem in social engineering.

2. Maurice Levine, M.D., *Psychiatry and Ethics* (New York: George Braziller, 1972), 23.

3. As an example, see Phil Laut, *Money is My Friend* (New York: Ivy Books, 1978, 1989).

4. Oliver Wendell Holmes, Jr., "The Path of the Law," *Harvard Law Review* 10 (1897): 457.

5. As one journalist recently observed about the medical profession, "More and more doctors are, in fact, thinking of themselves as business people. And some are doing very well at it." Victor Cohn, "Doctors and Dollars: Is Greed Eroding Care?" *The Topeka Capital-Journal*, Nov. 18, 1989, B1.

6. Bernd Guggenberger, *Das Menschenrecht auf Irrtum* (Munich and Vienna: Carl Hanser Verlag, 1987), 14–15.

7. See the discussion on "The Zones of Decision About Necessity" in Chapter 5.

8. While some tolerance must be allowed for mistakes made by competent professionals acting in good faith, it is hard to make clients suffer from these mistakes. Some mechanism must be developed that compensates such victims without categorizing the professional as incompetent or unethical.

9

Expanding Informed Consent

Instead of analyzing the primary dilemma as a problem of choosing between or balancing competing goals, one could view the ethical requirement of serving the client's best interest as a side constraint[1] rather than an end. Only when the side constraint has been met should the professional then move on to the strategic goals of achieving the client's ends and of implementing her own professional interests. Robert Nozick suggests that this idea of a side constraint is derivable from the Kantian principle that one must treat another person as an end, never as a means.[2] Alasdair MacIntyre forcefully makes the same point:

For Kant—and a parallel point could be made about many earlier moral philosophers—the difference between a human relationship uninformed by morality and one so informed is precisely the difference between one in which each person treats the other primarily as a means to his or her ends and one in which each treats the other as an end. To treat someone else as an end is to offer them what I take to be good reasons for acting in one way rather than another, but to leave it to them to evaluate those reasons. It is to be unwilling to influence another except by reasons which that other he or she judges to be good. It is to appeal to impersonal criteria of the validity of which each rational agent must be his or her own judge. By contrast, to treat someone else as a means is to seek to make him or her an instrument of my purposes by adducing whatever influences or considerations will in fact be effective in this or that occasion. The generalizations of the sociology and psychology of persuasion are what I shall need to guide me, not the standards of a normative rationality.[3]

In practice, this notion of treating the client as an end would require letting him control the choice. Thus, the client must be adequately informed and give his consent to the course of action suggested by the professional. The information provided should contain disclosure about the professional's self-interest that might cloud her judgment. This should also include a clear presentation of how the professional will be differentially compensated depending on the choices made by the client. In addition, there could be a recommendation that the client obtain an unbiased second opinion before committing himself to any serious course of action.

Stuart Twemlow, a psychiatrist friend, wrote me in relation to this problem:

My personal feeling is that both in medicine and in law the role of the patient/client is underplayed because of unconscious transference and countertransference factors. . . . I think that the patient/client can become informed, but not merely at the endpoint of a process, but needs to be fully informed from the outset and encouraged to question the attorney or physician. Our professions are loathe to allow this to happen. . . . I have found in medicine that a patient fully informed from the outset is frequently remarkably able to clarify his/her own needs and materially assist in borderline decisions.[4]

The professional-client relationship is one where this issue of using the other as a means rather than an end can work in both directions. We normally assume that the professional's expertise makes her dominant in the relationship. It is, however, the client who hires the professional and pays her compensation. There is not only the client who is subservient to the professional, but the client who views the professional as merely a tool. One pressure on the success horn, particularly for subordinate professionals, is that a client or supervisor will attempt to use the professionals they hire as instruments to attain un-ethical ends. Although this explains why many otherwise ethical professionals act improperly, does it explain why a professional would furnish unnecessary services? Would not a sophisticated and economically powerful client who can force a professional to act against her ethical desires be sophisticated enough to protect himself against overcharging or excessive services? There may be a trade-off. If the client gets wanted results from a professional's unethical conduct, would he be willing to allow overcharges? This seems to be a problem that has often occurred in defense procurement. There, a professional inside one bureaucratic or-ganization uses the services of a professional inside another. The two professionals can conspire to overcharge their clients. The larger the two bureaucratic organizations, the easier this type of conspiratorial overcharging could be. This is one context in which we have had much experience with the whistle-blower's dilemma. The structural change to prevent this type of unethical action would be better oversight and auditing systems.

CONSENT

Obviously, some form of consent is a threshold requirement in every professional relationship. Both the professional's right to compensation and her authorization to manage a client's affairs or to undertake some service for him arises from the notion of contract. Unless the threshold of legal contract is reached, profes-sionals are not entitled to recover compensation, nor would they have a defense to a legal challenge of unauthorized interference with the client's person, property, or freedom.

There are three distinct notions of consent I want to clarify: (1) assent, (2) informed consent, and (3) mutually satisfactory agreement. These move along a continuum from the bare con-tractual assent mentioned in the preceding paragraph, through informed consent, to a mutually satisfying agreement. The di-mensions represented on the continuum reflect both the degree of knowledge the client has and the degree of his interaction with the professional.

Assent is the least demanding form of consent. A legally en-forceable contract normally does not require much knowledge on the part of the client, merely assent in a situation where he could have obtained the knowledge if he had wanted to and if he had been diligent.[5]

Informed consent, which has been particularly stressed in health care situations, places an obligation on the professional to provide sufficient information so that the assent can be said to be based on all the necessary knowledge. The American Medical Association's Principles of Medical Ethics define informed consent as follows:

8.07 INFORMED CONSENT.

The patient's right of self-decision can be effectively exercised only if the patient possesses enough information to enable an intelligent choice. The patient should make his own determination on treatment. Informed consent is a basic social policy for which exceptions are permitted (1) where the patient is unconscious or otherwise incapable of consenting and harm from failure to treat is imminent; or (2) when risk-disclosure poses such a serious psychological threat of detriment to the patient as to be medically contraindicated. Social policy does not accept the paternalistic view that the physician may remain silent because divulgence might prompt the patient to forego needed therapy. Rational, informed patients should not be expected to act uniformly, even under similar circumstances, in agreeing to or refusing treatment.[6]

The legal profession is not more demanding on its members. Rule 1.4(b) of the American Bar Association's Model Rules of Professional Conduct provides:

A lawyer shall explain a matter to the extent reasonably necessary to permit the client to make informed decisions regarding the representation.

This requirement is elaborated in the Comment, which says in part:

[1] The client should have sufficient information to participate intelligently in decisions concerning the objectives of the representation and the means by which they are to be pursued, to the extent the client is willing and able to do so . . . .

[2] Adequacy of communication depends in part on the kind of advice or assistance involved. For example, in negotiations where there is time to explain a proposal the lawyer should review all important provisions with the client before proceeding to an agreement. In litigation a lawyer

should explain the general strategy and prospects of success and ordinarily should consult the client on tactics that might injure or coerce others. On the other hand, a lawyer ordinarily cannot be expected to describe trial or negotiation strategy in detail. The guiding principle is that the lawyer should fulfill reasonable client expectations for information consistent with the duty to act in the client's best interests, and the client's overall requirements as to the character of representation.

[3] Ordinarily, the information to be provided is that appropriate for a client who is a comprehending and responsible adult.

A *mutually satisfactory agreement* would go beyond informed consent by requiring not only that the professional give the client all the necessary information, but that she also help the client to reach a mutually satisfactory accord by trying to reduce to an insignificant point any misunderstandings and disagreements between the professional and the client about procedures, desired results, and obstacles in trying to achieve those results. This is the situation where neither professional nor client is being used as a means to the other's ends.

It should also be an important part of this understanding for the professional to assure that the client's expectations are realistic. The client should not only be aware of the risks that are possible from the external world in which the professional and client are acting, but also the risks inherent in the professional's limitations of competence and fallibility. To the extent that a client's dissatisfaction with a professional's services might be produced by unrealistic expectations, this is the point at which that problem should be dealt with.

A mutually satisfactory agreement, which is the ideal model, has both theoretical and practical problems. The theoretical difficulties are posed by the set of assumptions this model makes about the client's capacities. It assumes that the client is rational, mature, and sensible; that is, that he has the capacity to make sound decisions. Our whole interrelated theoretical systems of market economy, political democracy, and moral autonomy assume that adults have these sets of capacities and can use them. We know that for many, if not a majority of, adults, these assumptions are counterfactual. One of the strongest presentations of exceptions to this set of assumptions was made by Dr. Karl Menninger, who many years ago discussed the problem he says all surgeons and physicians are familiar with.[7] This is the self-destructive patient who insists for complex psychological reasons on having unnecessary surgery. He suggests that this is not an infrequent occurrence, and that such a patient will shop around among surgeons until he finds one who will perform the surgery. This poses in its starkest form the ethical dilemma faced by a professional who would profit from performing services that she knows are completely unnecessary, which may well be damaging to the patient, and yet the patient insists on the services.

Many clients often come to professionals in times of great stress. This situational pressure often inhibits the client's capacities to be highly objective, calm, and rational. One responsibility of the professional is to bring these qualities to the decision.

The practical difficulty is that the process by which a mutually satisfactory decision about services is reached calls for skills in counselling that many professionals do not have and also for time that many are reluctant to spend with a client.

Both the inhibited capacities of many clients and the reluctance of professionals to "waste" time in this process of reaching a mutual agreement push many professionals to dominate the decision.

PATERNALISM

Where a choice must be made about a future course of action based on the advice of a professional, there are three possible scenarios: (1) the professional makes the decision and informs the client, (2) the professional gives all the relevant information to the client, and the client makes the decision, and (3) a joint decision is reached that is mutually acceptable. These scenarios track closely our three types of consent. The ideal resolution is the joint decision. It is the client who must pay and who reaps both the benefits and costs of the choice. On the other hand, the professional must carry out the decision, so it must be a course of action that is within her competence and that is compatible with her personal and professional values. Therefore, the selected course of action must be acceptable to both.

There are problems with the ideal scenario. It is costly in time. The professional may be viewed as selling services, but more realistically she is selling a block of her time. A careful analysis of the influence of time cost on professional judgment would have to separate out self-employed professionals from those who are working in professional collectivities, such as law firms or medical clinics. In addition, a large percentage of professionals are salaried. Many doctors and lawyers have traditionally been self-employed independent contractors who can set their fees in whatever way they want. The analysis in this book works from such a model in which there is no intervening party between the professional and the client. Those employed on a fixed salary might take more time to make sure the decision to act was a mutually satisfactory joint one, unless, or course, the employer is cost conscious and does not want to pay his in-house counsel, the company doctor, or the employed accountant as much as he would if hiring a professional as an independent contractor.[8]

Using large chunks of a professional's valuable time to reach mutually acceptable preliminary decisions about whether services are needed and how they will be carried out calls not only for skills in communicating and educating, but the expenditure of time in a way that is economically less productive than prescribing services. Counselling about services is not as rewarding as the performance of the services themselves. We pay surgeons and trial lawyers more per hour than we do the diagnostician or the counsellor. Andrew Abbot has observed:

The professionals who receive the highest status from their peers are those who work in the most purely professional environments. They are the professionals' professionals who do not sully their work with nonprofessional matters, consultants who receive referrals only from other professionals. Barristers and modern-day surgeons are examples. Such high-status professionals may have exceedingly high incomes and extensive professional education, but their distinguishing mark is their work in purely professional environments.

That such workers should enjoy the highest status before their peers is not surprising. A profession is organized around the knowledge system it applies, and hence status within profession simply reflects degree of involvement with this organizing knowledge. The more one's professional work employs that knowledge alone—the more it excludes extraneous factors—the more one enjoys high status. . . . Conversely, the frontline professionals who make the first professional contacts with clients and whom the public usually venerates, are generally at the bottom of status ranks within their professions precisely because they work in environments where professional knowledge must be compromised with client reality.[9]

Not only do these factors of cost and status affect the way professionals and clients interact, but there is a strong tendency of professionals who are specialists with great prestige and training to feel that they can make better decisions for clients than clients can themselves. This paternalistic attitude is a serious problem in relations between individual professionals and clients and in the more generalized public reputation of the profession. Such a paternalistic attitude is usually inappropriate, because many decisions made by professionals are not just questions of technical skill and competence. Choices must incorporate the values and economic capabilities of the client.

The client of a lawyer may be risk-averse or risk-preferring. He may have a great need for harmonious relationships or a preference for conflict. Or he may be concerned with the financial bottom line, that is, the most efficient and cost-conscious decisions, or he may be interested in trying to protect or further principles or rights. To the extent that the professional's value preferences are different from the client's, the client's should prevail.

Different sets of value choices are faced by other professionals. For the patient seeking advice from a medical doctor, it may be the patient's pain threshold, concern about physical alterations such as change in appearance, cost-consciousness about treatment or a willingness to expend any amount, or aversion to taking drugs or to operations, and so on.

For the client of the investment counsellor, it may be the degree to which the client is risk-averse or risk-preferring, the age of the client, the number of dependents the client has, or other client preference factors.

If professionals have been strongly socialized to strive for financial success, it will have a major impact on how they relate to clients. They will select those specialties that permit the professional to provide high-skill, high-cost services, rather than the roles defined as counselling or educational. They will prefer to spend their time in objective technical performances, rather than "wasting time" in trying to persuade clients that a particular course of action is wisest, to say nothing of the even more time-consuming procedure of reaching a mutually satisfactory decision.

Professional paternalism, while frequently practiced, has been almost universally condemned. There are many situations, however, where it is justifiable, if not demanded. If the client is an infant or is incompetent, the professional certainly has paternalistic responsibilities. In fact the term *paternalism*, which has become pejorative, comes from the relationship of an authority over a child.

In emergency situations, a professional may well have to make decisions about what the client needs because there is seldom time, nor is the client often in a position to be informed and make a decision. This is not a context where a professional is likely to be providing unnecessary services intentionally, since she will be struggling to get the essential things done in a restricted amount of time. The greater danger in an emergency is that the professional may make mistakes because of time pressure, but that is unavoidable under any system of ethics.

Another situation where the professional is tempted, and perhaps justified, in taking over the decision is when an indecisive client just cannot make up his mind. There is a point beyond which more time spent on trying to get a client to come to a decision is inefficient from everyone's perspective.

When the professional makes a justified decision to begin acting paternalistically, she then most clearly takes on the character of a fiduciary and should be held to those responsibilities. Here, the duty to think only of the welfare of the client and to repress completely her own self-interest is at its strongest. She must act in complete good faith.

The problem that needs to be worked on by each profession is to develop better guidelines that define the situations where paternalistic intervention is justified, and those where it is not.

WHOSE AUTONOMY?

At the core of the definition of a professional is her claim for autonomy to practice her expertise. But should the claim for autonomy really belong to the client? My argument against professional paternalism and for the necessity of a mutually satisfying agreement is grounded on the role of the professional in protecting the autonomy of the client. A professional who is an agent for or fiduciary of the client then piggybacks her claim for autonomy on its utility in serving the welfare of the client, including defending and effectuating the autonomy rights of the client.

The argument that state regulation should not be used to strongly limit the autonomy of professionals can be defended on utility grounds. One such utility argument would be as a means to achieve the goal of enlarging the client's right to autonomy. Another would be the value of experimentation and risk-taking, not only for the individual client, but also to advance the expertise of the profession.

Both the state and the profession as an entity, when they claim power to regulate or constrain professional activity, are making a utilitarian claim as against claims of right the professional may make, not so much in her own right, but in the right of her clients. MacIntyre has suggested that individuals make their moral claims in terms of right, while bureaucratic organizations make theirs on claims of utility.[10] This is not to argue for the strong position that a right-based entitlement always trumps or wins over utility-based analysis. It is only to suggest that there are quite different bases for the analysis and that the right-entitlement of the client (and of his professional representative or provider) is quite strong.

Later, when we get to the question of whether the bureaucratic organization of the state or that of the professional group should better regulate practitioners to whatever extent is judged necessary, that choice should be made on utility grounds.

THE CONSEQUENCES OF EXPANDING INFORMED CONSENT TO REQUIRE A MUTUALLY SATISFACTORY AGREEMENT

If our conclusion is that the preferable solution for the dilemma is to encourage mutually acceptable decisions to be made between professional and client, changes are necessary. The first is that professional education must devote more time to training future professionals in the skills and processes of helping clients to make such decisions. This would be most difficult for members of those professions that are adversarial, such as law, or that regard themselves as technicians or scientists, such as surgeons, engineers, and architects. It would be easiest—in fact it is probably already a part of their repertoire—for the caring professions, such as psychologists and social workers. Another necessary change is to ensure that the compensation for counselling is similar to that for performing services, so that those professionals motivated primarily by economic incentives will not be tempted to hurry through the counselling stage to get to more lucrative uses of their time.

If our conclusion is that certain professions or individual members of any profession, because of values or personality types, are not capable of or are not interested in working with clients to help them make such mutually acceptable decisions about the necessity for professional services, this then argues strongly for separating the counselling from the performing roles and making sure that only those people with the competence and interest to do so are placed in the counselling role.

NOTES

1. Robert Nozick, *Anarchy, State, and Utopia* (New York: Basic Books, 1974) 28–35.

2. Ibid, 30–31.

3. Alisdair MacIntyre, *After Virtue* (Notre Dame, Ind.: University of Notre Dame Press, 1981), 22–23.

4. Letter dated November 6, 1989, from Stuart W. Twemlow, M.D., to the author.

5. The statement in the text assumes the standard arms length market transaction, which is both the legal and economic paradigm of contract. This ignores the possibility or probability that the court would classify the arrangement between professional and client as a fiduciary one, requiring substantial disclosure that would approach the requirement of informed consent before the court would say there is a contract. Clearly the extent to which the court will impose such an obligation will depend on the type of profession involved.

6. Rena A. Gorlin, ed., *Codes of Professional Responsibility* (Washington, D.C.: Bureau of National Affairs, 1986), 121–22.

7. Karl Menninger, *Man Against Himself* (New York: Harcourt, Brace & World, 1938), 259–78. Dr. Menninger suggests that it is not only the patient who may be incapable of making a rational decision, but the surgeon as well. He writes:

> When a patient submits to a surgical operation, at least two persons are concerned—the patient and the surgeon. Unconscious motives combine with conscious purposes to determine the surgeon's election to operate no less than the patient's election to submit to the operation. We generally assume that the conscious and rational motives of both are strongly predominant. For although it is obvious that surgery is a very immediate sublimation of sadistic impulses, it *is* a sublimation, and an exquisitely refined and very fruitful one which has already, in its relatively brief career, prolonged the lives and relieved the misery of millions. Of course, sublimations may break down, or they may be from the start only neurotic disguises; then the decision to operate, instead of depending upon the objective factors of infection, deformity, hemorrhage, and the like may depend upon a feeling of compulsive necessity. The ideal surgeon is neither anxious nor reluctant to operate; he is impelled only by the evaluation of reality factors. Unfortunately, careful inspection of surgical practice reveals the fact that surgeons sometimes operate for quite different reasons, such as those mentioned, i.e., a compulsion to do some cutting. Some surgeons are obsessed with the necessity for removing thyroid glands, others for removing the ovaries, still others for various surgical procedures upon the viscera. That such operations are sometimes scientifically justified there can be no doubt, but the way in which certain surgeons discover operative indications of precisely the same sort in patient after patient is so precisely comparable to repetitious neurotic behavior of other sorts that we have good reasons for suspecting that such surgeons are more neurotic than scientific.

Ibid, 260–61.

8. This assumes the client is not the employer, so the duties of fidelity are owed to a different person than the one paying.

9. Andrew Abbot, *The System of Professions: An Essay on the Division of Expert Labor* (Chicago: University of Chicago Press, 1988), 118–19.

10. MacIntyre, *After Virtue*, 68.

10

Restructuring the Professional Role(s)

If we do not wish to weaken the normative strength of the ethical obligation by redefinition, and if many professionals will not willingly take time to reach a mutually satisfying decision with a client, another possibility would be to adopt structural changes that minimize or eliminate the dilemma for individual practitioners. According to MacIntyre, Aristotle, who believed in the unity or harmony of the virtues, concluded: "It follows that conflict is simply the result of either flaws of character in individuals or of unintelligent political arrangements."[1] In this chapter, we explore the second alternative, that the ethical dilemma is created not by flaws in the professional's ethical character, but rather by unintelligent social and economic structures.

This chapter explores possibilities for organizational or social change, but any analysis has to realize how resistant social structures are to intentional change. Social structures are dynamic and changing, but in response to pressures and causes that we control only to a limited extent. Current structures of professions and professional activity are the products of tradition and history, of technology, and of how the professionals are embedded in relationships with other professions. As a result of this development, professions, particularly elite professions and their influential members, enjoy great social prestige, high incomes, and much power. A combination of inertia and special interest is likely to militate against significant and planned change coming from within any particular profession.

This problem of structural change can be analyzed from the perspective of society, of the profession, or of the individual practitioner. Society, or its formal representative, the government, has the broadest perspective and the greatest potential power. The profession in its limited sphere of jurisdiction over an area of expertise has almost as much power, but its concerns may be parochial. The individual professional, from whose perspective this book is primarily written, has little power over the structure, but some choice over where in the structure she can place herself to minimize the dilemma. For individuals, the structure of society or any subpart is a given. It must be understood, its tolerances and leeways evaluated, and a choice made about what stance to take toward and within the social structure.

In this chapter, we are concerned with altering or imposing external constraints or motivations, but relatively mild ones. The more severe sanctions will be discussed in the next chapter on compelling compliance by law. Since the ethical dilemma puts the professional in a choice situation arising from two lines of pressure that have relatively equal strength for the average professional, we need to consider changes that will alter the pressures. In Chapter 12, we will discuss ways of strengthening the ethical obligation, that is, the public service horn of the dilemma. Here, we consider ways to minimize or lessen the pressure forcing choice in favor of financial success or higher social status. One clear way to eliminate the conflict of interest is by separating the roles so that the counsellor has no self-interest in the result of the advice.

If the counselling and providing roles continue to be combined, we must reduce the financial incentive that pulls the professional toward giving advice adverse to the client's interest. This could be achieved either by placing the risks of bad advice on the professional or by removing financial incentives for giving poor advice. Although one can argue that this is already done through the medium of lawsuits for malpractice, the goal discussed in this chapter is not designed to impose penalties on the professional, but rather to remove the profits that would accrue from improper action.

SEPARATING THE PROFESSIONAL ROLES

The best structural way to avoid self-delusion or self-interest is to separate the person making the decision from anyone interested in the outcome. Lawyers are accustomed to discussing this separation when we evaluate the need to have an objective and nonpartisan judge or decisionmaker. A judge who has a personal interest in the outcome of a case either because he might be biased in favor of one of the parties or because the outcome might affect his own finances or the finances of a family member, must disqualify himself from hearing the case.[2]

We often forget that the lawyer is also an important decision maker. No dispute comes to a court for decision until a lawyer has decided it reaches the threshold of being a disputable legal issue. A decision that the case is not worth litigating resolves the putative controversy. Other professionals can be decision makers in the same way. Their advice, particularly if advising against any action or change of position, whether wise or not, is a resolution of the problem for the client. The primary dilemma, of course, arises from the reverse situation—the case where the professional advises the client to take action that requires her to provide expensive services. That situation requires the same freedom from self-interested bias as does the role of a judge.

If we acknowledge that the struggle between the professional ethic and the strong tendency of human nature to want to acquire as much wealth as possible[3] is a real difficulty facing practicing professionals, then counselling ought to be separated from providing services. The role conflict, and the resulting ethical dilemma, would disappear. The professional providing the services could then pursue her own self-interest in a rational and nonaltruistic manner.

While the legal profession in America has not experimented much with separation between counsellor and provider, the English legal system from which ours historically evolved has a well-known distinction between solicitors and barristers. Only barristers are permitted to appear regularly in the courts. Solicitors are the advisors to the clients and when litigation is necessary, it is the solicitor who hires the barrister and through whom the barrister is paid. Thus the barrister is insulated from the client, who has the solicitor to protect his welfare. In recent years, the British government under the leadership of Margaret Thatcher, herself a barrister, seriously tried to abolish this centuries-old system.[4] If such a proposal became law, there would then be only one class of attorneys, which means the British bar would be faced with the same dilemma as the American one.

The U.S. medical profession has tried various structural ways of separating counselling and performance. One was to institute the practice of the second opinion. Another was to develop diagnostic specialists, such as family practitioners, who are supposed to advise what medical services are necessary and then refer the patient to the appropriate specialist. There are three drawbacks that have prevented this separation from working well in practice.

First, there is reluctance by professionals to criticize the judgment or performance of fellow professionals. When a professional is hired to give a second opinion, this often leads to confirming rather than disagreeing with the original judgment. If counselling is separated from performance, the counsellor should go beyond just saying whether the services are necessary or not. She should also be available to supervise or evaluate the performance. Here, the counsellor would act much as an architect does when overseeing the actual construction work as agent for the owner. For this to work, counselling professionals must accept the responsibility to protect the welfare of the client. That would require them to be critical of performing professionals when their clients' interests call for it.

Second, the general knowledge of a diagnostician may be insufficient to make highly specialized decisions. For example, the family practitioner often sends the patient to the surgeon to make the decision about whether the operation is necessary.[5]

Third, separating the roles increases cost to the patient. Paying for a counselling opinion and then compensating the person who performs the services is more expensive than having the same person perform both roles. A related cost problem is that because of fear of lawsuits, both physicians will not trust the results or findings of the other without repeating their own tests, which would double the charges. Given the reluctance both of consumers and of health insurers to pay more for medical services than is absolutely necessary, this option to hire both an advisor and a performing physician has not been as widely used as might be desirable. Of course, the cost of counselling by disinterested professionals would be less to the public as a whole if it substantially lowered total cost by eliminating wasteful or unnecessary services.

Should we decide that the best solution is to separate the counselling and performing roles, there are some very practical problems. How do we get the professions to adopt and put such a change into practice? If the change is made, how do we develop alternative tracks of professional training for what are quite different sets of skills and expectations?

There may be an evolution or an increase in the separate role of counsellor occurring in our society. An example is the development of investment counselling. Another is family counsellors, who advise what more specialized assistance dysfunctional families might need. One might even cite the growth of popular advice columnists, such as Ann Landers, who often advise people with problems to see specified types of professionals. Instead of trying to force a separation between counselling and provider roles, the professions might just encourage the development and expansion of a counselling specialty. Clients would then have an option. If those who select counsellors are better served than those going to providers for advice, then this structural change might naturally evolve.

ELIMINATING MARGINAL PROFESSIONALS

If the serious ethical abuses are by marginal professionals, the structural solution would be to eliminate marginal performers. The root cause of marginal unethical activity is not lack of competence or of morality[6]; it is a problem of supply. Where the number of professionals exceeds the demand for their services, the pressure to provide unnecessary or excessive services is great. One solution is for licensing authorities to consciously limit licensed professionals to approximately the number necessary to meet the demand for professional services.[7]

A counterconsideration is that the elimination of marginal providers, particularly if we got it wrong on the side of undersupply, would restrict the choices available for those least wealthy. It would certainly minimize competition. There would be an increasing maldistribution of services, because scarce professionals would congregate in areas where wealthy patrons reside.

Actually, the problem of any particular marginal practitioner, with its attendant temptation to provide unnecessary services to meet her minimum financial requirements, tends to be short-lived. According to Andrew Abbott:

It has often been necessary for professionals to leave their careers and enter other professions. . . . At present such out-mobility is high in nearly every American profession except pharmacy and dentistry. By age 45, about 10 percent of a beginning cohort of pharmacists has left active practice, about 30 percent of physicians, 25 percent of lawyers, 30 percent of architects. Rates for clergy, engineers, social workers, and teachers are around 50 percent.[8]

Thus, there is no compelling need to structure entrance or admission to the profession in a way that eliminates marginal performers. They will withdraw voluntarily if they are unable to make an adequate living. The provision of unnecessary or excessive services to their few clients may postpone the marginal professional's decision to leave practice, but it cannot obviate that necessity altogether.

TRANSFERRING RISK TO THE PROFESSIONAL

Since the dilemma is caused in large part by the financial rewards accruing to those professionals who violate the ethical standard by performing unnecessary or excessive services, an obvious answer is to remove the reward or to create financial disincentives.

If the risk were placed on the professional by making her take the consequences of bad decisions, particularly the decision to provide unnecessary services, the seriousness of the dilemma would disappear. One significant issue of fairness raised by the problem addressed in this book is that the decisions are usually made by the professional, but it is the client who must pay the cost of an unwise choice, although naturally he would also reap the benefit of a wise decision. As long as the professional is not affected financially by an erroneous decision on whether services are necessary, there is no economic motive to reinforce the ethical directive.

One example of how this can be done comes from the lawyer's contingent fee. If the professional collects for her services only if she is successful, thus forfeiting the time and money invested in a losing cause, there is a strong economic incentive to figure the probabilities right and to bring only those cases where the chances of success are sufficiently strong to make it a wise investment for the professional. This unites the professional's self-interest and the interest of the client. Such a solution only works well on one side of the adversarial situation, since the defendant cannot use the contingency fee approach. The defendant is usually obligated to pay his attorney's fees, whether the case is won or lost.[9]

Is it possible to generalize the contingency fee procedure and to specify that professional remuneration will be available only for successful performance of services? Or perhaps to provide that a deduction of a substantial percentage from the normal fee can be made for unsatisfactory performance of services? The difficulty, if we try to generalize such economic incentives to all professional activity, is how to define a success that would activate the right to full compensation. We can easily envision situations where a client would want the professional to undertake a risky procedure even when the probabilities of success are low and would be willing to compensate her whether the procedure succeeded or not.[10]

Even if we could develop an acceptable standard of satisfactory performance for purposes of compensation, the fact issue of what constitutes unsatisfactory performance must be determined in some forum or another. To the extent that this issue would often be litigated, thereby raising costs and administrative expenses associated with making such a fact determination, it would require expending much of the savings that might come from eliminating unnecessary or questionable services.

A variant of this has been tried with some success in the profession of law as it relates to litigation. Rule 11 of the Federal

Rules of Civil Procedure requires that every pleading, motion, or paper filed be signed by at least one attorney of record and such signature constitutes a certificate by the signer that he "has read the pleading, motion, or other paper; that to the best of the signer's knowledge, information, and belief formed after reasonable inquiry it is well grounded in fact and is warranted by existing law or a good faith argument for the extension, modification, or reversal of existing law, and that it is not interposed for any improper purpose, such as to harass or to cause unnecessary delay or needless increase in the cost of litigation."[11] If any paper is signed in violation of this rule, the court shall impose upon the person who signed it, a represented party or both, an appropriate sanction, which might include an order to pay to the other party or parties the amount of the reasonable expenses incurred because of the filing, including a reasonable attorney's fee.

In general, this rule applies only to cases falling in the first zone, where services are clearly unnecessary. It is not likely to reach any of the more difficult contexts in the second zone, where the decision is a matter of judgment but most careful attorneys would advise against litigation.[12] There, the attorney has a good chance of persuading the court that her exercise of judgment was in good faith and based on a reasonable investigation. The other problem with the rule is that the violation may be said to be not only by the professional, but by the party represented (the client), and that party may be sanctioned. Such a sanction overlooks the serious problem of this study, which is that the professional may not be acting unethically or incompetently in relationship only to third parties, but also in regard to her client. Why should the client have to pay other parties injured by the professional's improper and often unauthorized activity?

PEER REVIEW

Another possible structural change, which could be used for most professions, has been pioneered in medicine. This is the concept of peer review.[13] Peer review committees have been created by hospitals to check procedures, particularly in surgery. Insurers may also utilize peer review committees to determine if the quality of care is adequate and the costs are not excessive. Since much health care funding is now done by the federal government through Medicare and Medicaid, there is a congressional directive requiring Peer Review of Utilization and Quality (PROs) to eliminate unreasonable, unnecessary, and inappropriate care.[14] According to one agency in the medical field,

> Peer review, simply, is the process of [The Kansas Foundation for Medical Care] looking over the shoulder of doctors, measuring their performance against accepted practices, and making sure that patients—and their insurers—get the care they pay for and need the care they get.[15]

Governmental insurers may contract for the use of such peer review agencies.[16]

Peer review seems an attractive structural change for dealing with the problem of unnecessary or excessive services. Clearly, professionals trained in the same area of expertise should better be able to understand and evaluate how fellow professionals exercise judgment and autonomy than would laymen, government officials, or members of different professions. Professionals, however, have a tendency not to be critical of one another unless there has been an egregious act of negligence. This means that such review may turn out to be fairly perfunctory. If not, peer review could have a chilling effect on professionals deciding whether to risk performing any procedures that are not conventional and accepted.[17] Thus, peer review may actually not be much protection to clients or patients, and at the same time might have an adverse effect on the way the profession is practiced.

There are multiple functions that peer review committees can perform. They can be used to determine whether services are necessary or not, whether necessary services were competently performed, and whether charges were reasonable and fair. Much of the motive for establishing peer review committees is based on the third function, cost containment. The use of such a structure has been pushed by third party payers like insurers and governmental agencies. The committee review may not only keep those services performed conventional and safe, but may constitute such financial pressure on performing services that it affects competence.

STANDARDIZATION OF DIAGNOSIS, PROCEDURES, AND COST

Cost pressure in the medical field has also led to developing standardized definitions of diagnoses, acceptable treatment procedures, and appropriate costs for these procedures. One approach is the Diagnostic Related Group ("DRG") concept:[18]

DRGs group patients primarily by principal (admitting) diagnoses, which are themselves categorized by body system into 23 systems or major diagnostic categories (MDCs). These groupings are then broken down into 467 separate categories by considering principal and secondary diagnoses, whether a surgical procedure was performed and, in cases where relevant, by further considering age, gender and discharge status. The purpose of this analysis is to yield groups of hospital patients, each covered by a distinct DRG, that require approximately the same consumption of medical resources.[19]

Such an approach assumes that professional categories into which problems are sorted can be identified, standardized, and used to answer questions about the necessity and cost of services. The notion of a self-fulfilling prophesy would imply that, whether the standardizations are realistic and determinable or not, the process of identifying such categories will produce standardization defined by normal or average professional judgment and activity.

Once the diagnostic categories have been accepted, they can be used to answer a series of questions. Was the service performed necessary or essential? Was the treatment excessive? Were the charges of the hospital or the physician excessive? Since these categories are used as a basis for payment or reimbursement by governmental agencies, physicians can be pressured to keep the cost of treatment within or below the guidelines, thus increasing income to the hospital.

In designing structures to control the provision of unnecessary services, care should be taken not to place the professional in a situation where there are conflicting pressures, thus creating a subdilemma along the success horn of our primary dilemma. Cost-containment measures like the DRG force doctors to use fewer tests, fewer days in the hospital, and fewer treatment procedures than would in their professional judgment be ideal medical care. On the other hand, legal regulation through malpractice actions,[20] or the possibility of them, would force doctors to use more tests, days of hospitalization, and medical procedures than are necessary so that in the event of litigation, the doctor can establish she went beyond the minimum or even the average treatment in making sure the patient was properly treated.

One might be tempted to say that the cost-containment system that pushes doctors to give less than ideal care and the legal malpractice regulatory activity that pushes doctors to give more than necessary care should, as a result of the two pressures, produce about the right level of care. Whether the resulting decision will achieve the best welfare of the patient and reflect the best professional judgment of good physicians is more a matter of chance and coincidence than good structural planning.

THE IMPACT OF TECHNOLOGY

Many of our more prominent professions are now dominated by technology and machines that started out as tools, but have now come to control how the practitioner functions.[21] By 1954, Jacques Ellul could already observe:

Technical progress today is no longer conditioned by anything other than its own calculus of efficiency. The search is no longer personal, experimental, workmanlike; it is abstract, mathematical, and industrial. This does not mean that the individual no longer participates. On the contrary, progress is made only after innumerable individual experiments. But the individual participates only to the degree that he resists all the currents today considered secondary, such as aesthetics, ethics, fantasy. Insofar as the individual represents this abstract tendency, he is permitted to participate in technical creation, which is increasingly independent of him and increasingly linked to its own mathematical law.[22]

Medicine, engineering, and architecture are examples of professions that are almost prisoners of their technology. Even professions such as law and journalism, which are not primarily technological, are increasingly controlled by their information technologies. This means not only that there is a great interdependence between professional and machine, but also that much

of the technology and machinery is so complex and so inter-
woven with other parts of society that machines must function
or the society will collapse with enormous damage. When a bank
computer is down, most transactions cannot take place. If one
small component does not function, a space shuttle flight must
be aborted. A single malfunction at any place in a power grid
can start the process that throws an entire region of the country
into darkness.

Machines are expected to function flawlessly. The human component in the technology must also function flawlessly. When
an unexpected accident occurs and an investigative team tries
to assess the cause, the ultimate blame is often "human error,"
an indication that we expect the human to be as free of error as
a well-designed machine.

One problem created by the dominance of technology in a
profession is that it encourages an expectation that the better
the technology is, the fewer (human) errors there will be. And
yet increasing complexity makes it likely that there will be
more breakdowns and that the damage caused will be much
more extensive. Neither the human participants in the technology
chain nor the complex technology itself can maintain the level
of flawless performance our society has come to expect of technology. One structural change of great importance is to design
mistake-friendly technology and procedures—in other words, to
expect mistakes and to plan ways to minimize their damage when
they occur.

The more complex the technology and the expertise of professionals become, the more there will have to be specialization,
which will require much more collaborative effort by many different kinds of professionals. This increases the possibility of
oversights and incomplete planning. Once there has been an unexpected loss, we are treated to the sight of the different professionals on the team blaming each other. In the wake of the
collapse of a balcony at the Hyatt Regency hotel in Kansas City
that killed a number of people, there was difficulty in identifying
whether it was the architect, the structural engineer, the general
contractor, or the supplier of materials who was responsible.[23]
All were part of a complex technical machine. No single one was
clearly accountable.

CONCLUSION

The present structure of the profession leaves a large area of autonomy or discretion to individual professionals, and it is within that area of professional freedom that abuse occurs. A central component of the concept of professionalism is that the individual should enjoy the maximum possible autonomy in the performance of her activities. This arises from her expertise, her training, and the fact that the professional's duties are not primarily mechanical or routine, but call for the exercise of judgment.

Each of these possible structural changes discussed in this chapter calls for a negative or constraining impact on the autonomy of individual professionals. The separation and apportioning of counselling and services between different members of the profession, or the use of peer review boards after the fact of performance, are regulatory constraints on individual autonomy, but at least they are regulation by people sharing the same training, expertise, and professional values.

There are three possibilities: (1) complete and unregulated autonomy with the hope that internalized notions of competence and ethics will assure that autonomy is exercised wisely; (2) regulation and supervision by the profession; and (3) governmental or social regulation of the professions by use of legal mechanisms. If the public believes that large-scale abuses by autonomous professionals are occurring, the public choice will likely be between requiring strong professional monitoring or moving to governmental regulation. A cynical public view about the ethics of individual professionals spills over into an equally strong suspicion of the integrity of the profession as a whole. If the professions do not take strong steps to not only police their members, but also to ensure that the public believes that they are doing so, we will probably see increasing governmental policing.

Before advocating substantial structural changes, we need better empirical evidence to use in deciding between the lesser of two evils or the greater of two benefits. Do the advantages of holding marginal or unethical practitioners to complying with minimal or conventional standards of practice, with the consequence that talented and honest professionals may well have to hew close to that same line, outweigh the loss to society that comes from innovative, risky, and unconventional activity of autonomous, competent, devoted, and gifted professionals? Ideally, we would like to be able to constrain the less talented professionals by structures that require them to practice conventionally by accepted standards, while leaving the gifted free of these constraints. It is extraordinarily difficult to design and administer such a two-tier structural framework.

NOTES

1. Alasdair MacIntyre, *After Virtue* (Notre Dame, Ind.: University of Notre Dame Press, 1981), 147.

2. For example, The California Code of Judicial Conduct provides under Canon 3, "Judges Should Perform the Duties of Their Office Impartially and Diligently," the following:

C. DISQUALIFICATION.

(1) Judges should disqualify themselves in a proceeding in which their disqualification is required by law, or their impartiality might reasonably be questioned, including but not limited to instances where:

(a) the judge has a personal bias or prejudice concerning a party, or personal knowledge of disputed evidentiary facts concerning the proceedings;

(b) the judge served as lawyer in the matter in controversy, or a lawyer with whom the judge previously practiced law served during such association as a lawyer concerning the matter, or the judge or such lawyer has been a material witness concerning it;

(c) the judge knows that, individually or as a fiduciary, the judge or the judge's spouse or minor child residing in the judge's household, has a financial interest in the subject matter in controversy or is a party to the proceeding, or any other interest that could be substantially affected by the outcome of the proceeding;

(d) the judge or the judge's spouse, or a person within the third degree of relationship to either of them, or the spouse of such a person:

(i) is a party to the proceeding, or an officer, director, or a trustee of a party;

(ii) is acting as a lawyer in the proceeding;

(iii) is known by the judge to have an interest that could be substantially affected by the outcome of the proceeding;

(iv) is to the judge's knowledge likely to be a material witness in the proceeding;

(2) Judges should inform themselves about their personal and fiduciary financial interests, and make a reasonable effort to inform themselves about the personal financial interests of their spouses and minor children residing in their households.

Thomas D. Morgan and Ronald D. Rotunda, eds., *1989 Selected Standards on Professional Responsibility* (Westbury, N.Y.: Foundation Press, 1989), 347–49.

3. This is not to take a position about whether competitive wealth seeking is inherent in human nature or is merely culturally instilled through socialization. Rather, it simply recognizes that this is a strong drive in most contemporary professionals.

4. Fenton Bresler, "Thatcher vs. The British Legal System," *Los Angeles Times*, April 2, 1989, Opinion, Part 5, 2.

5. Can we separate the judgment of whether an action ought to be taken from the question of who will be performing those services? Are the two so intertwined that they cannot be separated? When the person is giving the second opinion, or the diagnostician is trying to answer the question of whether a service is needed, does she not have to face the strategic question of what services are going to be performed and by whom? Do we sacrifice the interplay of these two questions when we separate the functions or roles away from a single person?

6. Lack of competence or morality may play a role in rationalizing a decision by a marginal professional to proceed when one ought not to do so.

7. Obviously one difficulty here is that the demand for professional services is not fixed, but is elastic, and is very difficult to measure before the demand for services is made.

8. Andrew Abbot, *The System of Professions: An Essay on the Division of Expert Labor* (Chicago: University of Chicago Press, 1988), 132.

9. Thus, there is a lack of symmetry in the way the incentives work. The plaintiff is encouraged to sue, the defendant to settle. One temptation for the defense bar is to hide this factor from their clients, so that the defendant will continue to finance the litigation and increase their fees.

10. If we try to create an exception for these types of cases by permitting the client to choose to pay for risky procedures that turn out unsuccessful, we would open up the possibility of routine use of this escape device to erode our attempts to tie compensation to success.

11. Federal Rules of Civil Procedure, Rule 11 (as amended effective Aug. 1, 1987). See Chapter 11 for a more complete description of the operation of Rule 11.

12. See discussion of zones of decision in Chapter 5.

13. For a general discussion of peer review boards, their operation, strengths and weaknesses, see Barry R. Furrow, Sandra H. Johnson, Timothy S. Jost, and Robert L. Schwartz, *Health Law* (St. Paul: West Publishing Co., 1987), 417–40.

14. See 42 U.S.C.A. §§1320c-1320c-12.

15. Vickie Griffith Hawver, "Peer Review Agency Checks Care Quality, Costs," *The Topeka Capital-Journal*, Nov. 4, 1989, B1.

16. Ibid.

17. This was the claim made by the plaintiff in *Union Labor Life Ins. Co. v. Pireno*, 458 U.S. 119, 123 (1981), where a chiropractor claimed the use of a state-created chiropractic peer review committee by a third party paying insurer to decide whether the services were necessary and whether the charges were reasonable violated the Sherman Antitrust Act and contended "that the members of the Committee 'practice ' "antiquated" ' techniques that they seek to impose on their more innovative competitors."

18. See Furrow, Johnson, Jost, and Schwartz, *Health Law*, 455–64.

19. Ibid, 456–57.

20. See discussion of professional malpractice in Chapter 11.

21. This idea is developed in great detail in Jacques Ellul, *The Technological Society* (New York: Vintage Books, 1954, 1964).

22. Ibid, 74.

23. The flavor of this dispute, the vast sums of money involved, and the difficulty of deciding can be gleaned from reading *Crown Center v. Occidental Fire & Cas. Co.*, 716 S.W.2d 348 (Mo. App. 1986), a case where the various insurers of the owner were disputing which of them had the obligation to defend and pay the losses.

11

Compelling Compliance by Law

The line between ethical duties and legal duties is not always clear. There is a substantial overlap between the realms of ethics or morality on the one hand and of the law on the other. The classic distinction is that legal duties are those carrying state-imposed sanctions. If so, the ethical duty of a professional not to perform unnecessary services may often be a legal duty.

If our conclusions at this stage of the analysis are that the ethical obligation is clear and properly stated, but that many professionals are intentionally or carelessly violating that standard, then we are faced with what is essentially a compliance problem. A common solution is to compel conformity with the norm by use of law. The ethical obligation becomes a legal one. This represents the use of an extreme external motivator, namely, legal sanction. As long as we use only ethical exhortation or economic rewards and penalties, we recognize that the professional has a choice. One may choose to be unethical. One may elect to forego economic advantage. One is not entitled to choose to disobey the law. Of course, one can violate a legal obligation and may well get away with it, but that is a different matter. Getting away with breaches of the law is a matter of luck, not something one is entitled to.

The imposition of state-enforced sanctions has impact on the form and content of the way duties or obligations are stated. There is a policy in the law, and often a constitutional requirement, that any rule that carries legal sanctions must be specific enough to inform the obligor what he or she must do in order to be in compliance.[1] Ethical obligations that carry no government sanction can be stated in more general or aspirational terms. Those parts of ethical codes that have the force of the law tend to be stated in terms of specific rules. Such a formulation makes it possible for those regulated by such rules to assume that technical or literal compliance with the rules is all the ethical obligation they have. If the promulgators of ethical codes and legal (ethical) obligations want to avoid this attitude of technical conformity with the rule, the principles must be stated with fairly general standards, such as "good faith," "reasonable judgments," and "community standards of practice." When these standards carry legal sanctions, the professional has difficulty in predicting the exact content that these terms will be given by the administrative agencies or courts charged with their enforcement. The professional who wants to be sure to comply will then be led to very cautious practice that is unquestionably within the boundaries of the guidelines. The undesirable consequence of either rule-specific norms or flexible guidelines if they carry serious legal sanctions is more routinized performance and less innovative or risky practice.

LICENSING REGULATIONS

In most professions, the practitioner must receive a license from a state-authorized board. One stage on the road taken by occupations that are trying to achieve status as professionals is to apply for and achieve state licensing.[2] The license requirement is supposed to guarantee that all members of the profession are competent. Thus, it is arguably designed to be a protection for the public, who can rely on the fact that the professional has been certified as competent by the state. The function of state licensing that carries with it the power to enjoin the performance of professional tasks by nonlicensed professionals may equally be to protect the occupational territory from encroachments by others. Licensing determines not only who will be in the profession, but who will be kept out.[3] Many professional codes demonstrate how important this function of licensing may be by placing a duty on the licensed professional to help prevent unauthorized practice by unlicensed providers. For example, Canon 3 of the American Bar Association's Model Code of Professional Responsibility provides: "A Lawyer Should Assist in Preventing the Unauthorized Practice of Law."[4] It is somewhat less explicit, but clearly implicit, in the American Medical Association's Principles of Medical Ethics, which provides:

3.01 NONSCIENTIFIC PRACTITIONERS

It is wrong to engage in or to aid and abet in treatment which has no scientific basis and is dangerous, is calculated to deceive the patient by giving him false hope, or which may cause the patient to delay in seeking proper care until his condition becomes irreversible.

Physicians should also be mindful of state laws which prohibit a physician from aiding and abetting an unlicensed person in the practice of medicine, aiding or abetting a person with a limited license in providing services beyond the scope of his license, or undertaking the joint medical treatment of patients under the foregoing circumstances.[5]

Our concern is with those who are licensed and what protections the law makes available for their clients. The license is not only issued for technical or professional competence, but also for the requisite moral character. The license can be revoked for unethical conduct, which would include providing unnecessary services, or at least a pattern of doing so.[6] This power to suspend an existing license is rarely used, particularly when the questionable activity is the provision of unnecessary services.

If we move from the administrative sanctions of the licensing boards to the sanctions imposed as a result of court action, there are a number of possible legal theories on which such sanctions might be based.

CONTRACTUAL OR WARRANTY THEORIES

The relationship between professionals and clients is created by contract. The contract may be express or implicit. The existence of a contract is, of course, essential to the professional being able to recover compensation for services, and is also a defense against a charge of unauthorized interference with the person, property, or liberty of the client.[7] Whether the contractual arrangement is express or implied, there is little doubt that professionals undertake to perform services competently, and that failure to do so should make them liable for breach of contract. This is certainly so *a fortiori* if the professional states or warrants that the services will be successful and will achieve the objectives of the client. If there is an express warranty that a result will occur, the professional may also be liable on a breach of warranty theory.[8]

A well-known example is the case of *Sullivan v. O'Connor*.[9] The plaintiff was a professional entertainer who was unhappy with her nose, which she felt was too prominent. The defendant, a plastic surgeon, promised that an operation on the nose would make it more attractive. After three operations, the nose in fact was markedly uglier and no further operation would improve her appearance. The jury found that the defendant had promised or warranted that the operation would be a success. The court held he should be liable for all expenses incurred by the plaintiff in obtaining her operation and for the pain and suffering caused by the operation. This was not labelled unnecessary surgery, nor should it be, since the plaintiff understood what was involved and elected to undergo the operation; the doctor's liability was based on the incompetent performance of appropriate surgery. The performance of unnecessary surgery could be considered just as much a breach of the doctor's undertaking to perform services competently as could the negligent performance.

Increasingly, whether it is expressly stated in a contract or not, the courts imply a duty of good faith.[10] Both the obligation to be competent and the duty to exercise good faith would seem to encompass the duty not to perform unnecessary services or at least services that the client does not want or has not agreed to.

FRAUD

If the professional makes any statement that the services are necessary or essential, and the client can later establish that the statement was untrue and known to be untrue, the client may sue the professional in tort for deceit.[11] Except in egregious cases, it is hard to prove that the professional's statements were made with an intent to deceive. To establish such an intent to deceive, the injured client must negate the alternative explanations that the professional was incompetent but acting in good faith, or that she just exercised temporary poor judgment.

One interesting variant of the use of fraud or warranty theories of liability applicable to the lawyer engaging in litigation on behalf of a client is found for in the operation of Rule 11 of the Federal Rules of Civil Procedure:

> Every pleading, motion, and other paper of a party represented by an attorney shall be signed by at least one attorney of record in the attorney's individual name, whose address shall be stated. A party who is not represented by an attorney shall sign the party's pleading, motion, or other paper and state the party's address. . . . The signature of an attorney or party constitutes a certificate by the signer that the signer has read the pleading, motion, or other paper; that to the best of the signer's knowledge, information, and belief formed after reasonable inquiry it is well grounded in fact and is warranted by existing law or a good faith argument for the extension, modification, or reversal of existing law, and that it is not interposed for any improper purpose, such as to harass or to cause unnecessary delay or needless increase in the cost of litigation. . . . If a pleading, motion, or other paper is signed in violation of this rule, the court, upon motion or upon its own initiative, shall impose upon the person who signed it, a represented party, or both, an appropriate sanction, which may include an order to pay to the other party or parties the amount of the reasonable expenses incurred because of the filing of the pleading, motion, or other paper, including a reasonable attorney's fee.[12]

This compels the attorney to make certain warranties or guarantees about her actions in litigation and authorizes sanctions to protect the opposing party harmed by filing an unnecessary action. This has been widely used against the trial lawyer's version of performing unnecessary services, the filing of lawsuits without merit. "[J]udges had issued more than 1,000 published opinions analyzing Rule 11 and finding actions frivolous under it. They have levied fines that have escalated so that now they sometimes exceed $1 million in a single case."[13]

The rule is highly controversial and is being reexamined by an advisory committee of the Judicial Conference. Among the complaints made are that it discourages civil rights cases, that it is costly because the expense of litigating Rule 11 and determining its applicability may equal or exceed the cost of litigating the trivial suit, and there is little uniformity because judges differ about what is trivial or without merit.[14]

From the perspective of this book, the problem with Rule 11 is that it does not protect the client and may even expose him to having to pay the penalty to the other party. Lawyers (and lay people as well) in analyzing the adversarial context of litigation tend to identify the client and lawyer as having the same interest and thus the client does not need to be protected from the lawyer. This position is written into Rule 11. The thesis of this study questions that assumption. It is only when the lawyer explains to the client that the suit is not meritorious and the client consents to it, or insists on its prosecution, that the client should be responsible to the other party under Rule 11.

PROFESSIONAL MALPRACTICE

Although it has been used much more for incompetent or sloppy performance of what usually were necessary services, the more probable legal theory in cases of unnecessary services by a professional is negligence, or professional malpractice.

Professional men in general, and those who undertake any work calling for special skill, are required not only to exercise reasonable care in what they do, but also to possess a standard minimum of special knowledge and ability. Most of the decided cases have dealt with physicians and surgeons, but the same is undoubtedly true of dentists, pharmacists, psychiatrists, attorneys, architects and engineers, accountants, abstracters of title and many other professions and even skilled trades.[15]

A judicial determination that services were unnecessary carries the implied judgment that competent professionals would not have advised that the services be performed and therefore the professional who advised and performed the services was engaged in professional malpractice.[16] Related to the issue of unnecessary services is the problem of misdiagnosis. This is more nearly akin to classic malpractice negligence actions, but if the misdiagnosis has to do with what services are necessary, the damage done to the client is the performance of those services.[17]

While legal remedies for the prevention of incompetent or unnecessary services are available, they have until recently been used sparingly, partly because of administrative difficulties and partly because of deference to professional judgment and supervision. The lax supervision by professional organizations may well have provoked the growth in professional malpractice actions, which is clearly a form of state regulatory activity.[18]

Professional malpractice actions are not a particularly efficient or satisfactory way to determine and supervise whether the members of a specialized profession are performing their duties competently and ethically. The first disadvantage is that such actions are costly, an important factor motivating the medical malpractice reform movement in the last decade and a half. If a major factor in condemning the provision of unnecessary or excessive services is the wasted expenditure of resources by the client and by society, expensive measures for redressing this problem merely compound that difficulty. There are large legal costs to obtaining a determination that a professional was acting improperly. Through liability insurance premiums, these become a part of the cost of providing services to the clients and patients of all professionals, whether they be competent and ethical or otherwise.

The second disadvantage arises from administrative difficulties in leaving the determination of whether services were competently performed in the hands of a lay jury.

The wide gap in knowledge between the lay person and the professional is maintained by the profession's effective monopoly over a stock of theory and skill. Professionals, of course, master the intellectual bases of their profession. In addition, they see that no one else does by controlling the channels of education and research. As a result only professionals are equipped to judge the work of professionals.

The monopoly of competence is the foundation for the professional autonomy.[19]

Even with the help of expert witnesses, those not trained in the profession have difficulty in understanding the complexity of the technical professional problems and the subtleties of the judgments brought into question.

There is another subtle but critical administrative drawback to the use of legal sanctions to compel compliance with what are primarily obligations of professional ethics. If we assume that legal obligations are appropriate to regulate the zone where clearly unnecessary services are being provided—an area of intentional immoral activity—but are inappropriate for the cases falling within the second and third zones—the gray areas where reasonable, competent professionals might disagree[20]—the problem in the real world is keeping the categories apart. The distinguishing characteristics are factual. Was the professional acting competently, reasonably, and ethically? This must be determined in some forum for official fact finding. An aggrieved client may in good faith believe that the professional was acting according to criteria that place the case in the first category of intentional wrongdoing, whereas the professional believes she was acting in a way that makes it a matter of discretion and sound judgment. The possibility of this claim being made carries costs to the professional of lost time, damage to reputation, and litigation expense, even if the professional is ultimately vindicated. The fear of such claims leads honest and competent professionals to be overly cautious to avoid the possibility of the claim being made.

THE RANGE OF TOLERANCE FOR HUMAN ERROR

Once professional duties to clients are translated into legal duties, courts or administrative boards have serious problems in applying those standards. How do we build into the rules and their application the range of tolerance appropriate for the occasional misjudgment of an otherwise ethical and competent professional? The professional claim to autonomy may in part be based on fear that such distinctions could not be soundly made. Medical doctors have been particularly concerned about this due to the spate of malpractice actions over the past several decades.

Since a civil legal action must be initiated by a party who feels he has been aggrieved, we might say this is left to the judgment of the client. In smaller communities where professionals and clients know each other socially as well as professionally, many clients can make reliable decisions about how ethical and competent the professional is. They might well then be understanding and not make claims for normal errors and misjudgment. On the other hand, social pressure arising from such community relationships could equally inhibit a genuinely aggrieved client from making a protest or from bringing any legal action.

In the more alienated urban areas of our contemporary world, there are neither inhibitions on clients bringing such actions nor much of a basis for making sound judgments about whether an error falls into the zone of tolerance. In such an environment, the process of trying to reach a mutually satisfying understanding at the outset of the relationship is of great importance in establishing realistic expectations, indicating the risks, including the risk of error, and creating a trusting relationship where the client is less likely to want to sue the professional if the services fall below the ideal.

The distinction between a professional who in good faith makes an excusable error in judgment and the unethical practitioner who should be regarded as violating legal standards could be made by the judge or trier of fact in the course of litigation. There are, of course, large costs associated with this way of defining the zone of tolerance. Given predictable biases against certain professions and practitioners as well as sympathy for injured parties, there is no certainty that an objective decision would be attempted or made.

If the claim is made that a zone of tolerance must be created for occasional lapses by ethical and competent practitioners, we must still face the problem of why their clients should suffer or bear the risk of loss in those cases. That is where the institution of liability insurance is most useful. It is unfortunate that a condition for its use must be a finding that the professional acted wrongfully or negligently. What ought to be developed is a middle category, a finding that the professional did not act improperly, but there should still be insurance compensation for the person who has suffered because of an excusable professional misjudgment.

CONCLUSION

The difficulties with eagerly grasping for legal sanctions as the solution to our dilemma are partly theoretical, but mostly practical. If we divide professionals into three categories, (1) those who always act ethically and never provide unnecessary services, (2) those who are totally indifferent to the ethical duty and provide all the unnecessary services they can persuade clients to pay for, and (3) those who are committed to being ethical, but through the exercise of bad judgment, through carelessness, or through caving in to intense pressure, occasionally provide services that are unnecessary or excessive, then it is this third category that we are most concerned about. I assume this category includes the bulk of all professionals. No one should feel any qualms about imposing legal sanctions on those practitioners in category (2) who intentionally act unethically. The problem is the use of legal sanctions on those who occasionally act improperly through carelessness.

Standards for which legal sanctions are to be used ought to be stated in a very different fashion than ethical obligations. They must reduce complex problems of judgment to simple questions of right and wrong. The law, of course, is often compelled to use standards rather than clear rules, the most obvious being our general standard of reasonable care, the core concept of our law of negligence. The generality and vagueness of that standard have produced the vast bulk of our civil litigation in tort. That standard would have been totally unworkable in the modern world without the development of the institution of liability insurance, which means that the actor who violates that general standard is usually insulated from having to pay any penalty himself, but probably is also not stigmatized as a law violator. The tort and liability insurance system is increasingly used to regulate professional conduct through malpractice actions, and the problems with that approach when applied to medical doctors have produced a political and economic crisis for our society.

Perhaps the most serious theoretical and practical problem in the use of legal sanctions is its impact on professional autonomy. I am reminded of the introductory paragraph in Harold Havighurst's *Nature of Private Contract*, where he wrote:

Merlin, the magician, had the task of educating the young Arthur, destined to become a great king. At one point in the course of the instruction, T. H. White tells us, Merlin came to feel that it would be good for his pupil to learn about the habits of a number of animals and insects, and that the best way to teach him would be to transform him for a period into each one of these creatures so that he could have a personal experience of their various ways of life. Pursuant to this plan, Merlin one day changed Arthur into an ant. Living as an ant in a community of ants, the boy found that he was part of a well-regulated social system. At appropriate points he found signs posted which read "Everything not forbidden is compulsory!" This was apparently true in the ant society of Arthur's time; and since insect societies are said not to be progressive, I see no reason to doubt that it is true in the ant societies of today. Every action is prescribed.[21]

Havighurst's point was that there is no room in such a society for private contract. Mine is that there is no room for discretion, freedom, individuality, or autonomy. Do we want professionals to be mechanical followers of clearly defined procedures and rules, or do we want them to be people capable of and willing in unclear or undefined situations to use such judgment and skill as appear best to them at the time? If our aspirations or expectations for good professionals are the latter, we should be cautious about turning the ethical obligations of professionals into legal ones.

NOTES

1. For a well-known argument that this is a moral requirement for any legal system, see Lon L. Fuller, *The Morality of Law* (New Haven: Yale University Press, 1964), 35–36, 38–39.

2. An example of an occupational group that should be faced with the dilemma discussed in this book is those who hold themselves out as "financial planners." They are not currently licensed, so anyone can claim the title and perform the functions. See Anita Miller, "Financial Planners," *The Topeka Capital-Journal*, Jan. 21, 1990, B1:

> Financial planning became a buzzword in the 80s; the number of those hanging out shingles as planners escalated dramatically.
> But the 1990s likely will bring more regulation to the industry, a move some hope will limit those who can designate themselves as planners and close the loopholes for consumer abuse.

Obviously one way to protect the public is to install a licensing procedure.

3. One consequence of this creation of an occupational monopoly has been a proliferation of self-help books that purport to train the prospective professional client how to perform professional tasks for himself, such as how to make his own will, to diagnose and treat many of his ailments, to sell his own home, to cure his psychological problems, and so on. A not insignificant percentage of the profits of all commercial publishers in the past few decades have come from such books.

4. Thomas D. Morgan and Ronald D. Rotunda, eds., *1989 Selected Standards on Professional Responsibility* (Westbury, N.Y.: Foundation Press, 1989), 27.

5. Rena P. Gorlin, ed., *Codes of Professional Responsibility* (Washington, D.C.: Bureau of National Affairs, 1986), 109.

6. See *In Matter of Winkley*, 243 Kan. 753, 763 P.2d 620 (1988), where an attorney was disbarred who told the client that he had filed a wrongful death action when he had not, and the statute of limitations ran on the action so the client could no longer recover.

7. Without consent, a professional performing services is liable in tort for assault and/or battery, if injury is caused to the person, and for conversion if damage is done to property. See *Ipock v. Gilmore*, 326 S.E.2d 271 (N.C.App., 1985) for a case of a surgeon being held not to have available the defense of consent when an operation was extended beyond that which the patient had agreed to.

8. See *Burns v. Wannamaker*, 333 S.E.2d 358 (S.C.App., 1985), where the court permitted an action against a dentist who had warranted that dentures would fit, when in fact they did not.

9. 363 Mass. 579, 296 N.E.2d 183 (1973).

10. This gets much of its support form the Uniform Commercial Code, particularly §1-203. The code does not apply expressly to personal services contracts, but courts have by use of analogy been expanding the contract theories of the code to other area of contract.

11. An egregious case of intentionally bad advice aimed at promoting the welfare of the advisor, rather than the client is *Anderson v. Knox*, 297 F.2d 702 (9th Circ. 1961), *cert. denied*, 370 U.S. 915 (1962). This case involved an insurance agent. Other cases of fraud actions brought against professionals include *Harkins v. Culleton*, 544 N.Y.S.2d 432 (Sup., 1989), a doctor; *Watts v. Cumberland County Hospital*, 330 S.E.2d 256 (N.C.App. 1985), a doctor; and *Callahan v. Callahan*, 127 A.D.2d 278, 514 N.Y.S.2d 819 (App. Div., 1987), a lawyer.

12. Federal Rules of Civil Procedure, Rule 11 (as amended effective Aug. 1, 1987).

13. Stephen Labaton, "Courts Rethinking Rule Intended to Slow Frivolous Lawsuits," *New York Times*, Sep. 14, 1990, B12.

14. Ibid.

15. William Prosser, *Handbook of the Law of Torts*, 4th ed. (St. Paul: West Publishing Co., 1971), 162.

16. For an interesting example, see *Black v. Littlejohn*, 325 S.E.2d 469 (N.C. 1985), where a patient sued a surgeon for performing an unnecessary hysterectomy. The Food and Drug Administration had approved the drug Danocrine to treat plaintiff's condition more than two years before the surgery was performed. The problem before the North Carolina courts was whether the statute of limitations on malpractice actions ran from the time of the surgery or from the time that the patient learned that a drug was available that made the surgery unnecessary.

17. For an egregious case of such misdiagnosis leading to the performance of unnecessary services and severe damage because of it, see the fact situation in *Sibley v. Board of Supervisors of Louisiana State University*, 446 So.2d. 760 (La. App., 1983).

18. See John Kultgen, *Ethics and Professionalism* (Philadelphia: University of Pennsylvania Press, 1988), 91, where the author says: "These are strong demands indeed—to be entrusted with vital interests and to be immune from judgment. They can be justified only if institutions ensure that professionals do not abuse their powers. Society is forced to rely on the conscience of the individual and such lax controls as the profession exercises to ensure that he will be trustworthy. It also must trust the profession to have its house in order."

19. Ibid, 84.

20. See Chapter 5 for a discussion of these zones of decision.

21. Harold C. Havighurst, *The Nature of Private Contract* (Littleton, Colo.: Fred B. Rothman & Co., 1981), 3–4.

12

Professional Education and Professional Ethics

If the problem is not structural, that is, something we could change by restructuring roles or by redefining professional obligations, the only possible solution is to try to influence the attitudes that control professionals when they make choices. Professional education is the route to that end. Can students be taught to be ethical? Can professionals learn to be relatively detached, so they will notice when self-interest colors their judgment? Should we educate them not only about what technical competence requires, but also how to factor ethical responsibilities into their judgments? If a student is inclined to be decent and thus is open to being guided, the ethical attitudes and values transmitted by professional education become crucial.

It has sometimes been urged that schools cannot make students more ethical. Whether they will act ethically or not is said to turn on what their character and moral positions are. These are formed long before they come to professional school. Medical educators have recently suggested that before applicants come to medical school, they should be carefully told what ethical expectations are placed on doctors so that those feeling uncomfortable with these requirements could choose not to become doctors.[1]

If the primary cause for unethical conduct is lack of knowledge about appropriate guidelines and applications, education should improve the ethical conduct of professionals of good character. It will not solve the problem of the amoral or immoral student on the way to becoming a financially successful professional, in other words, the profit seeker masquerading as a professional.

Professional schools are the entrance gates to the professions. We could try to eliminate people of immoral character at this entry stage. In order to do so, admission committees would require more information than they presently do—information particularly hard to obtain—in order to make judgments about moral character. Admissions committees would then be faced with making difficult and controversial judgments. However, administrative problems and the difficulty of judgments are not sufficient justifications for abstaining from this responsibility.[2]

Alasdair MacIntyre has argued that a true system of ethics has a "threefold scheme in which human-nature-as-it-happens-to-be (human nature in the untutored state) is initially discrepant and discordant with the precepts of ethics and needs to be transformed by instruction of practical reason and experience into human-nature-as-it-could-be-if-it-realized-its-telos [natural end]."[3] The human nature, while hardly untutored, brought by most students to professional schools reflects the dominant cultural values of ambition, competitiveness, desire for material success, and craving for high social status. On the other hand, professional human nature should be service-oriented, trustworthy, and loyal to the welfare of the client. The task of ethical instruction in the professional schools is to use "practical reason and experience" to transform the personality already formed by the dominant culture and brought to professional school into a professionally responsible personality. That is a formidable responsibility.

THE PROBLEM OF THE PROFESSIONAL EDUCATOR

Lon Fuller and William Perdue ended the first paragraph of their celebrated article "The Reliance Interest in Contract Damages" with the comment that "Nietzsche's observation, that the most common stupidity consists in forgetting what one is trying to do, retains a discomforting relevance to legal science."[4] It is just as applicable to the education of lawyers and other professionals. We must decide on our goals and keep them clearly in mind.

What the goals should be of professional education in the matter of ethics depends on how the questions raised in the preceding chapters are answered.

If we decide that the professional roles need to be restructured by dividing the counselling role from the performing role, then students must learn to perform the roles separately.

If ethical obligations must be treated as equivalent to legal rules and be enforced by legal sanctions, such as loss of license or civil fines, then students must be trained in the content of the rules, the types of sanctions imposed for infractions, and under what circumstances the sanctions will be applied. My impression is that most courses in professional ethics are taught that way. This is particularly true in legal ethics, which is only to be expected, because most professors who teach legal ethics will naturally bring attitudes and perspectives from other law courses into a legal ethics course. A major criticism of this approach is the narrowness of its focus and its general perspective on what ethics means. The difficult ethical issues are those in the gray areas, those ambiguous zones where right and wrong are much more matters of professional attitudes rather than of clear rules. There are serious ethical aspects to how technical judgments should be made, and codes of rules can be dangerous. Professionals who find no clear rule on the problem may assume there are no ethical issues to be considered.

If our goal decision after considering the questions in the prior chapters is that external motivations and sanctions carry undesirable side effects, such as too severely limiting professional autonomy or pushing professional practice toward safe, conservative, risk-free activity, then the role for professional education should be to create, encourage, or develop internal motivations. These should ensure that most professionals in advising clients make ethical judgments that can be defended as being both technically and ethically sound. In other words, we must help our students develop into persons of professional character who practice ethical virtues.

Selecting this goal of the creation of internal ethical motivations requires not merely that different things be taught, but that different methods or levels of education be used. Limiting education to the communication of information, whether it be about the technical aspects of professional practice or about the expectations for ethical practice, is at most a guarantee that the information will remain at a conscious or cognitive level only, where it can easily be lost. It will not become a part of the organic or total professional personality.

How does one drive learning to the point where it becomes a part of the student's person? The first requirement is that the lessons to be taught must be a part of the teacher's person. Professional educators are often early and important models for students, not merely of professional technical competence, but also of professional character.

While the aspiring professional will have as her customer or client the person needing the specialized expertise of the profession, the professional educator has the student as her client. Almost all the questions raised in this book can also be addressed to the professional educator. Do teachers provide unnecessary or excessive services for the payment made? Do they develop mutually acceptable solutions to the learning problems of the students? Do they treat students paternalistically?

Most professions have long had codes of ethics, a sign that they are at least willing to formally address ethical issues. It is only relatively recently that codes of ethics have been proposed and adopted for professional educators. The first code of ethics for lawyers was adopted in Alabama in 1887, and the American Bar Association first promulgated and adopted a code of ethics in 1908.[5] In contrast, the American Association of University Professors' *Statement on Professional Ethics* for university professors was endorsed in 1966.[6] The American Association of Law Schools formulated a code of ethics for law professors in 1989.[7] The absence of a code of ethics does not mean that professors have been acting unethically. The promulgation of a code probably indicates, however, that there have been complaints inside and outside the professional group about unacceptable practices, and that the members of the profession are beginning to think seriously about what their ethical obligations are and should be.

One clear ethical dilemma facing the professional educator is a role conflict between the professor's role as teacher and her role as scholar or researcher. Professional educators often argue that these roles are complementary, not conflicting. Few students have been persuaded by these arguments.[8]

Another dimension of this role conflict is between two models or goals that teachers have for students. They may view themselves as educating the next generation of teacher-scholars, or as educating the next generation of professional practitioners.[9] Educators may trot out the familiar argument that these roles are complementary and the same training should satisfy both. The training for the roles, however, is not at all the same, and a standard complaint of professional students is that they are being trained to be scholars or researchers, not practitioners.

A further role conflict for professional educators is the tension between being a teacher and a practitioner. This is a long-standing problem faced by many deans of law schools and probably of other professional schools as well. How much time may a full-time professor spend in practice or consultation for compensation? The standard answer has been that the practice, if done to improve or hone the professor's skills or improve her expertise, is acceptable, or even desirable; practice done just to enhance income is unacceptable.

Perhaps one could say then that the professional educator is faced not with a dilemma, but a "trilemma." What percentage of her time ought to be devoted to teaching, what to scholarship, and what to practice? Attempts to resolve this "trilemma" with formal time allocation rules have been made, but not with much success. The guidelines have to vary from institution to institution and from one professor to another. Using law schools as an example, a national law school that educates many future professors would naturally place more emphasis on research and scholarship, while a state law school preparing the local bar and supported by state funds might be expected to do more consulting work, particularly on questions of local law reform. Instead of trying to formulate general rules to control allocation of time or the resolution of conflicting expectations, it should be a matter of autonomy subject to broad guidelines and ethical constraints.

A professional educator is hired as a full-time teacher. Her clients are the students. Her ethical obligation is to promote their welfare. Therefore, she should be expected to justify any activities that are not directly related to servicing those clients as bearing some rational relationship to that end.

Professional educators have a double ethical obligation—those of the professional herself and those of the model for future professionals. To serve the second role well, she must satisfy the first and be observed to satisfy the ethical obligations of that role.

It is a moral responsibility of educators to serve as ethical models, but this is an obligation of older or senior practitioners as well. This tradition is old in those professions that formerly used an apprentice system for preparing the next generation. The master was not only a fount of craft or professional expertise, but also a model of guild character. Today when a professional-school graduate, under the guidance of older professionals, is making the transition from student to practitioner, the model of the supervisor is just as important as that of the teacher in ultimately forming professional character. Unless both teachers and senior practitioners complement and support each other in stressing and demonstrating appropriate ethical attitudes and character, the young professional may perceive an option to be amoral or indifferent about ethics.

THE SCHOLAR-TEACHER AS CONSCIENCE OF THE PROFESSION

The dominant view of the professional educator held by many if not most teachers, by much of the profession, and by the public is that the teacher-scholar is a conservator and developer of the technical competencies belonging to the expertise of each profession. In fact, the best practitioners often know as much or more of the technical skills and knowledge as any academic. Practitioners also contribute much to the development and improvement of these skills and knowledge.

Teacher-scholars have a different and much more important role, which arises from two aspects of their status in the profession. The first arises from their position in the professional organization or hierarchy. As academics employed by a university, they are insulated from the pressures of dealing with lay clients and from competing for an uncertain income. They are also insulated from the incessant demands on time suffered by highly successful practitioners. A large block of their time is available for reflection and detached thought. Professional educators can be more objective about the role of the professional and of the profession, and can do so from a broader and more idealistic perspective. Most members of the profession meet other professionals in a competitive atmosphere that often has the quality of jurisdictional or turf battles. Academics meet other professional academics in a somewhat more cooperative fashion and can think about boundary lines and allocation of problems among the professions on a more objective and rational basis. Professional school faculties can be, although often are not, more open to other professions. A medical school faculty can use a lawyer to teach legal responsibilities of the doctor, a biologist to teach biology to medical students, or a psychologist to teach about the mental side of illness, whereas the medical profession would allow none of these to practice medicine. A law faculty might have an economist, a philosopher, or a psychiatrist on its faculty. A business school may have lawyers, economists, accountants, and mathematicians (at least as teachers of statistics).

This enables scholar-teachers to deal in more detached and rational ways with issues of the definition of professional role and the utility of professional services to society and to individual clients. Naturally, any educator-teacher who is trained as a professional cannot totally escape the pressures of professional imperialism, that is, to try to bring more social problems under the domination of their own profession. The medical school faculties had as much or more to do as any other members of their profession with bringing alcoholism and mental problems under the control of medical doctors by defining these as diseases. Law faculty had much to do with bringing tax problems under the control of the legal profession, although there is an ongoing battle over this turf with accountants. The teacher-scholar is the member of the profession who has the best chance to rise above professional parochialism and impart to the profession an objective and ethical analysis of the profession's activities.

The second aspect of the educator's role is her responsibility to conserve the traditions and history of the profession and contribute to their development. The service horn of the dilemma, the commitment to public service, is a product of this tradition and history. The teacher who educates the next generation of practitioners fulfills the role of the parent who, in psychoanalytic theory, provides the content of the superego, the conscience.[10] The parent inculcates in the child a list of dos and don'ts that become internalized as the conscience. The professional educator should perform this role for the aspiring professional.

If the scholar-educator defines herself as the trainer of technical competencies only, she abdicates this critical role of conscience and conscience-builder to the profession. She then bears a substantial part of the responsibility for the amoral attitude of the profession.

If the dilemma of the individual practitioner in choosing between service and success is a daily balancing of the strengths of these two competing aims, the professional educator, by abdicating her role of conscience-builder and ethical trainer, weakens the weight along the horn of service and makes it easier for the choice to be swamped by the cultural pressures along the success horn.

THE CHOICE BETWEEN PURITY AND HONESTY

Professional educators may well disagree about how to discharge their responsibility in ethical education. Some feel they should hammer home the ethical obligation without any compromise or discussion of conditions or contingencies. Their role is to fix the ethical injunction as firmly and purely as possible as an ideal or norm. The presentation of the nitty-gritty details of practice and the sordid compromises that often must be made could weaken the norm. This should be left until after graduation to be learned from fellow practitioners and supervising professionals.

Other educators believe that honesty requires them to present the reality of professional practice, rather than some idealized picture. This entails discussing all the pressures that might be brought to bear toward selling unnecessary or excessive services in order to be a success.

My preference is this second alternative of honest presentation of reality. The ethical obligation at the level of ideal is largely unproblematic and accepted at least formally by almost all professionals. The difficult questions are how strong the ethical obligation is against competing obligations, and how it should be applied in the myriad of real contexts of professional judgment. These issues cannot be addressed if teachers do not draw an honest picture of the real dilemmas of practice.

Of course, I believe teachers have a responsibility to present both positions or levels of discourse—the ideal and the honest reality. Teachers must also worry about the relationship between the two and getting the balance right. Not only is the amount of time spent on each level important, but the tone or stress on the ideal is critical. The student should always leave any discussion with the feeling that the ethical obligation is weighty indeed and in all cases of doubt the balance of the scales should always be slanted in the direction of following the ideal. Any tendencies of the student to be cynical, amoral, or indifferent about ethical obligations must be met head on.

CURRICULUM

What ought to be done in professional education to improve professional ethics is controlled in large part by our tentative answers to questions posed in preceding chapters. If our solution to the dilemma is to encourage more careful informed consent through mutual decision-making procedures, professionals need to be trained in the techniques of fully informing clients, understanding their needs, and working toward mutually satisfying agreement. If our solution is to separate counselling from performance roles, then we need to identify which students will go into the different roles and to prepare appropriate ways of training for the different roles.

Special Courses or Integration Throughout the Curriculum?

There has been a debate in legal education, and I am sure in most professional education, about whether there ought to be special courses in professional ethics and in the traditions, history, and mores of the legal profession, or whether ethical training should be a responsibility of all teachers and ought to be integrated into the entire curriculum. That debate has been largely resolved in favor of special courses in legal ethics. The special course, now required of all law students, is a guarantee that every student has been exposed to some ethical training. The American Bar Association and state bar associations have been very sensitive about ethics training since the days of Watergate, with its widespread publicity about the immoral and illegal activity of so many members and advisors of the Nixon administration, most of whom had been trained as lawyers.

The integrated approach, which was tried experimentally in some schools,[11] foundered on a practical problem: how to ensure that all faculty, including the majority who were primarily concerned with the technical training of lawyers, devoted the required time to the ethical problems associated with their course.

If almost every decision about rendering services to a client has an ethical as well as a technical side, then teachers should include ethics in every discussion of the use of professional judgment. Students make judgments about the importance of issues by the amount of time and stress placed on them. The relegation of these problems to an occasional mention in the typical course and then to a specialized course on professional ethics, constituting perhaps 2 or 3 percent of total curriculum time accurately indicates the importance many educators give this issue.

The Problem of Role Differentiation and Educational Tracking

If our preferred resolution of the professional's dilemma is to separate the roles of counselling and providing services, that should be reflected in the professional schools. Oftentimes, professional students do not specialize or commit themselves to any particular specialty during their formal training. Specialization occurs only after they become full members of the profession. Part of the task of the professional school is to show them the range of possibilities from which they can choose their own specialization, as well as to familiarize them sufficiently with all the branches of knowledge belonging to the profession so they can work with other specialists in a cooperative way.

The education of a counsellor and diagnostician on the one hand and a performing specialist on the other should be different. This is not just a matter of training, but also of personality types. Not all persons have the capacity to be empathetic listeners, effective transmitters of professional knowledge to lay people, and wise counsellors. If a task of professional education is to help get round pegs into round holes rather than square ones, some career guidance is necessary. If we are committed, as almost all American higher education is today, to a laissez faire approach to career choices,[12] those choices by individual students will seldom be made on the basis of fit between personality and role, but on the basis of the important reward in our society, that of compensation. The dilemma between service and success rears its head even at this level. Presumably, the most aggressive, ambitious, and intelligent will select the best-paying specialties, which are not in the counselling track. This will produce some serious misfits between talents and jobs, unless one is willing to accept the tacit belief held by much of our population that the performance role of the professional is the tough, hard-nosed one that requires the talents of our strongest people, while the counselling roles are softer and thus are appropriate places for the less talented.

If we decide to have two tracks of training, one for performers and one for counsellors, an interesting question is how diverse the paths should be. A pure performer, if she is to have any contact with the client, must have some of the communication skills and counselling ability of the formal diagnostician or advisor, as well as an understanding of the role of the counsellor and what has been done in that capacity. Conversely, the counsellor must understand the technical problems of the performer well enough to advise the client and to supervise or evaluate how well the services have been performed.

Ethical Stories

In older and more traditional societies, education in ethical character and expectations was done through story-telling.[13] In this culture, we are most familiar with that tradition through the parables of Christ, but other religions also use stories or parables as a way of ethical training. While it may be fashionable in academic circles to downplay anecdotal evidence because anecdotes are subject to sampling bias, we do use stories all the time to educate. These stories are usually not a part of formal curricula, but are an informal part of the introduction of young people to the ways the profession is and ought to be practiced. But what stories are told in professional education and in professional gatherings? Do they not almost always emphasize financial success and often extol amoral, if not immoral, activity? Where are our stories and examples of ethical practice? Where are our parables illustrating good professional character?

It should be the responsibility of professional educators and of professional leaders to collect, preserve, and transmit stories about ethical activity. These stories should be told in a way that suggests they are not extraordinary events and that the heroes of such stories are not superhuman, but ordinary professionals who practice virtues and exhibit character available to and expected of all members of the profession.

Somewhere between the modelling done by living members of the profession and the storytelling behind ethics training lies the territory of the legendary heroes of the profession. A whole generation of lawyers was reared on the legend of Clarence Darrow, celebrated much more for his character as a defender of the underdog than for his competence as a litigator, although that competence was to be admired as well. A newer generation could celebrate Ralph Nader, who almost single-handedly created the role of consumer watchdog. In medicine, there was for a long time the towering figure of Albert Schweitzer, one of the world's great musicians, who gave that up to minister to the sick in Africa. Generations of scientists have followed the example of Albert Einstein, a genius who remade much of physics but did not try to obtain great material wealth. Equally impressive models for natural scientists were Louis Pasteur and Marie Curie. These people are still legends, but they are ceasing to be "living" legends, because their character, as distinguished from their technical achievements, is no longer being celebrated by living professionals. If their fame is still being sung, it is not a music that seems to reach our young aspirants.

There is enormous value in using the living models of teachers or practitioners and the idealized models of the profession's legendary heroes, but Stuart Twemlow has raised for me a cautionary note:

> Using ideal examples is of course very popular in our platonic culture, oriented to Forms, in Plato's sense. As a psychoanalyst, I see many of the problems associated with idealizing, which clinically is considered to have as its underpinning the unconscious emotion—hostility, but I'm also aware that idealization can be a vehicle for learning. And more particularly, for setting high aspirations. . . . I agree that students these days are not as influenced by ideals and values within their professions. Perhaps this is a side issue, but in my view science and technology, particularly positivist science that idealizes logic and rational outcomes has a pernicious impact. . . . I believe that the idealization of logic and technology has caused a general reduction in the investment in human relationships and in valuing and caring for human life, so that in many ways our society has become and is becoming far more like a dehumanized machine than perhaps many of us want to realize.[14]

The model or legendary professional should be used aspirationally, but not to create impossible goals that the student dismisses as unachievable.

Training Toward Judgment

One aspect of the dilemma, the ease of rationalization toward self-regarding economic actions amid the complexity of professional judgments, rises from the fact that the ethical standard is simple and clear, but the contexts in which it must be applied are complex and varied. This applies not only to ethical problems, but also to the problems of professional competence of most professions in any but the most routine tasks.

There is a widespread misapprehension among lay people, but also among some professionals, and in my experience, most students in professional schools, that the expertise of the professional consists of mastering the technical skills and learning the technical knowledge that is the monopoly of the particular profession.

There is a tension in each profession about whether the problems facing the professional should be structured or defined as difficult to resolve, as complex, and as calling for judgment, or whether they should be pictured as standard types of problems with clear-cut routine resolutions. Most students and many practitioners prefer well-structured, orderly, neat problem definitions and clear solutions, because they are easier to master and to apply. One could criticize that desire as not being reality-oriented, because the human problems professionals must face are often messy, multilayered, and not easily classified. There is a utility to the profession from defining problems as complex and calling for judgment. It makes it easier to defend the profession's territory as one of special expertise, which requires monopoly and autonomy.

The craft or art of genuinely competent professionals is much more that of knowing which skills and knowledge to use under what circumstances; in other words, their problems are defined as questions of judgment and discretion. That judgment requires knowing much about the client who is asking for the service and adapting professional skill and knowledge to satisfactorily solving the client's problems, not only as defined by the professional, but as defined by the client. Looked at this way, the ethics of protecting the best interest of the client are part of the issue of genuine professional competence. Therefore, preparing the professional student for the realm of professional practice requires ethical training to be integrated at every step of the process of judgment.

CONTINUING PROFESSIONAL EDUCATION

In a rapidly changing world where the demands for the expertise of the professional are expanding or contracting and the social contexts in which professionals perform are constantly altering, training the professional in the professional school at the onset of her career is not enough. As the professions of law and medicine and many others have recognized, professional education is a life-long task. Programs of continuing education developed either by professional associations or by professional schools are generally conceived of as aimed at keeping the practicing professional up to date on new developments in the areas of professional knowledge and skills. My thesis is that, as social conditions change and professional knowledge and skills evolve, the ethical judgments that fit those contexts will also change. This means that continuing legal education, which ought to be education in the newer problems of professional judgment, must contain discussions of the changing ethical dimension of such judgments as an integral part of this education.

THE PROBLEMS OF SUPERVISION OR OVERSIGHT

The profession has, or should have, an abiding interest in the ethical conduct of its members. The lowest ground on which this interest can be placed is one of public image or perception of the profession, the issue of public relations. If the public perception of the profession is that it is unethical or dishonest, all members of the profession, however upright as individuals they might be, will suffer. Such a perception not only diminishes the respect the profession and its members are held in and the willingness of the public to patronize the profession, but concomitantly this perception will increase demand for governmental or lay supervision or regulation. Both law and medicine have suffered and are suffering from such a lowered perception of their integrity. Lawyers have been used to it for at least a century and a half. Nearly everybody knows and is fond of quoting the Shakespearian injunction that we should kill all the lawyers or the Dickens line, "The law is an ass." Many are familiar with Carl Sandburg's poem, "Why Does a Hearse Horse Snicker?" Medical doctors have been faced with this problem of low professional esteem only in the past few decades.

A more exalted justification for professional oversight over its practitioners' ethics is the duty to protect the more ethical members from competition by the less ethical practitioners. If powerful and wealthy segments of our population believe that members of the profession are for sale, that is, they can be persuaded by bribes or extra compensation to act in unethical ways, that often puts pressure on honest but ambitious professionals to meet that competition. Professional organizations have an obligation to not permit the least ethical members to act in such profitable but dishonest ways, and thereby set the standard for everyone. This not only creates a bad public relations picture, but pressures decent members of the profession to abandon their ethics.

The most exalted ground for the responsibility of the profession to oversee the ethics of its practitioners is that a profession is distinguished from an occupation by the fact that it is dedicated to ethical service to its clients. If it does not live up to that willingly assumed obligation, it forfeits any claim to autonomy and control over its area of expertise.

Professional educators belong not only to the profession they are training their students for, but also the profession of teaching. The teaching profession, particularly in higher education where almost all professional education occurs, has an extraordinarily strong commitment to the autonomy of their profession as teachers, through the protection of academic freedom. They must often defend that autonomy against professional organizations that want to control the curriculum on what will be taught and how it will be taught. This has been a particularly difficult problem in legal education. The primary accrediting agency has been the American Bar Association, the professional association of lawyers. The leaders of the profession have a natural feeling that they understand the professional environment, the problems faced by lawyers, and the skill and knowledge they need as well as, if not better than, law professors.[15] They will often, through accreditation requirements, control the curriculum and ways of teaching. An even stronger constraint on the autonomy of legal educators is the bar examination that is under the control of the highest courts of the various states. Since the graduates of a law school will not be licensed unless they can pass the bar examination, a major constraint on the design of any curriculum will be the knowledge and attitudes law students must acquire to satisfy the various boards of bar examiners.[16] Since very few law schools are so local that their graduates all stay in the same state, the constraints are complex and multiple, and curricula must be designed to satisfy a number of boards of bar examiners. This effectively narrows in very substantial ways the freedom of any law faculty.

Professional faculty thus are multiprofessional and have a commitment to protecting the autonomy of both their occupational role, that of the professional teacher, and their student's occupational role, that of the profession for which they are being educated. The best way to protect the autonomy of the profession they are educating the students for is to prepare them to exercise autonomy and discretion in socially responsible ways.

NOTES

1. See Lawrence K. Altman, "The Proper Time to Tell Doctors What Will Be Expected of Them," *New York Times*, Oct 3, 1989, C19. The precipitating cause for this suggestion was the refusal of some medical doctors to treat patients with AIDS.

2. Professional schools do not completely avoid this responsibility, but usually limit exercise of the power to cases where there is hard evidence, such as a criminal conviction for some act involving moral turpitude.

3. Alasdair MacIntyre, *After Virtue* (Notre Dame, Ind.: University of Notre Dame Press, 1981), 50–51.

4. Lon L. Fuller and William R. Perdue, "The Reliance Interest in Contract Damages," *Yale Law Journal* 46 (1936): 52.

5. Henry S. Drinker, *Legal Ethics* (New York: Columbia University Press, 1953), 23–24.

6. American Association of University Professors, *Policy Documents & Reports*, 1984 ed. 133–34.

7. Association of American Law Schools, *Memorandum 89–92*, Nov. 22, 1989.

8. For a more extended discussion of this issue, see Banks McDowell, "The Audiences for Legal Scholarship," *Journal of Legal Education* 40 (1990): 261.

9. These models may differentiate elite schools from average schools, since the elite schools train the bulk of professional educators.

10. Stuart Twemlow suggests that my definition of superego in this context is too limited. He wrote that "the superego is a precipitate of a whole variety of internalized experiences during childhood, including cultural and societal norms, the experiences from authority figures like teachers, grandparents, and material that the child reads; influence from a variety of sources, including the parents but not exclusively parents." Letter dated October 30, 1990, from Stuart W. Twemlow, M.D. to the author.

11. This observation is based on personal experience. Following Watergate, when it was clear that law students needed more ethical instruction and the bar associations were recommending, or even requiring, such instruction, Boston University School of Law, where I was then on the faculty, opted for the integrative approach. Each professor was required to devote the equivalent of one hour out of the semester's requirement of the typical three semester hour course's forty-two hours to ethical training. After two years, the program was abandoned because of the difficulty of monitoring its administration. Instead, a special course was instituted.

12. I am not advocating forcing people into careers against their will. The middle way between total autonomy and conscription is to offer much more help and guidance to students trying to find their proper niche. For this to be genuinely effective, compensation for the different roles should be more equalized so that those being guided in certain directions will not feel economically underprivileged.

13. MacIntyre, *After Virtue*, 114.

14. Letter from Stuart W. Twemlow dated October 30, 1990, to the author.

15. There is no claim in this book that that assumption is unrealistic. The teacher's expertise is in conveying those skills and knowledge, and teachers occupy a more detached and objective position from which to view the problems and practices of the profession. Well-designed professional education requires cooperation and a mutually satisfying agreement between profession and teacher, not unlike the ideal understanding between professional and client discussed above in Chapter 8.

16. For a criticism of professional group control of what is university education, see Robert Paul Wolff, *The Ideal of the University* (Boston: Beacon Press, 1969), 9–27.

13

Conclusion: The Right Balance

Rather than offering premature or simple solutions to complex problems, this book is intended to explore a vital issue for all professionals and to show its complexities and difficulties. Developing simplistic solutions to difficult problems may be worse than not doing anything, but ignoring serious problems by pretending they do not exist is equally indefensible.

One way to evaluate the problem is to consider the interests that are in conflict. This involves at a minimum the interests of the professional and of the consumer. This analysis is helped by an insight from Karl Polanyi:

> Once we are rid of the obsession that only sectional, never general, interests can become effective, as well as of the twin prejudice of restricting the interests of human groups to their monetary income, the breadth and comprehensiveness of the protectionist movement lose their mystery. While monetary interests are necessarily voiced solely by the persons to whom they pertain, other interests have a wider constituency. They affect individuals in innumerable ways as neighbors, professional persons, consumers, pedestrians, commuters, sportsmen, hikers, gardeners, patients, mothers or lovers—and are accordingly capable of representation by almost any type of territorial or functional

association such as churches, townships, fraternal lodges, clubs, trade unions, or, most commonly, political parties based on broad principles of adherence. An all too narrow conception of interest must in effect lead to a warped vision of social and political history, and no purely monetary definition of interests can leave room for that vital need for social protection, the representation of which commonly falls to the persons in charge of the general interests of the community—under modern conditions, the governments of the day. Perhaps because not the economic but the varied interests of different cross sections of the population were threatened by the market, persons belonging to various economic strata unconsciously joined forces to meet the danger.[1]

The professional has an economic interest in maintaining the autonomy and monopoly of expertise free of regulation or supervision, whereas the client has an interest, both economic and social, in not being subject to an unsupervised professional environment in which exploitation of clients is easy. Professionals, who have such an interest in unregulated freedom in their own fields, will be clients of other professionals and then interested as consumers in supervised professional activity.

There is also a profound interest of society as a whole. This is that the resources of the society should be used efficiently to achieve the welfare of the whole population. The services of the professions are intimately related to various welfare needs of the population. The medical profession promotes health, the legal profession promotes justice, journalism promotes truth, teachers promote wisdom and enlightenment, architects and engineers promote technological and mechanical progress.

Society must be concerned about allocation of social and economic resources among the professions. The professions are engaged in a competition for resources. While the provision of unnecessary services on an individual or profession-wide basis enhances the share of resources coming to one profession over others, this is a distortion of fair allocation across the whole range of social needs.

All professionals might be said to share an interest in maintaining professional freedom and thus be expected to band together under a platform of protecting professional autonomy.[2] If professionals are developing into a new class in our society with common economic and social interests, then one would expect a class solidarity in the protection of important class interests, most particularly that of professional autonomy.[3] Even if that were to happen, the strength of all professional groups when united might not be enough to counteract the pressure of all nonprofessional consumers.[4] It is not likely, however, that all professional groups share the same wish for autonomy. Members of subordinate professions like nursing and accounting have little interest in supporting the autonomy of medical doctors, lawyers, and corporate managers if that autonomy will be used to keep them in a subordinate position. But even the doctors and lawyers, the elite of the professions, cannot unite in such an effort.[5] The current malpractice controversy presents such a clash. The doctors, supported by the liability insurance industry, are trying to protect the professional autonomy of doctors.[6] Trial lawyers, supported by certain consumer groups and cost-conscious health insurers, are attempting to subject doctors to more stringent social control and financial responsibility, particularly when they carelessly injure a patient.[7]

The professions should share an interest in a united front to maintain professional autonomy. That position must be based and defended on a broader ground than mere economic interest. The autonomy necessary for professionals in the exercise of their expertise and judgment can best be maintained when there is trust by the rest of society. That trust must not only be requested—it must be earned. The professions should be united, which means that the more prestigious professions must not only expect subordinate professions to support their claims for autonomy, but must also offer the same respect and autonomy to those professions. This would require that much of the competition for social status and power be relaxed, not only between the various professions, but also between the more successful members of the profession as against less prestigious members.[8] The professions need to become genuinely fraternal to enlist broad professional support in this struggle to preserve professional autonomy. Ultimately the professions, if they are to prevent overly strong social regulation, must establish the fact that professional autonomy serves not only the interests of the professions, but those of all people.

The autonomy of the professions and of individual professionals can be justified in one of two ways. The first is the one often used throughout this book, which is that the profession possesses special expertise or competence that cannot be judged or evaluated by someone who does not possess the same background. Although a strong version of this premise might be used to justify the conclusion that the individual members have a right to total autonomy in the practice of their profession, a more rational position is that the professions are the ones that have the competence (and the duty) to regulate or monitor individual practitioners. This is clearly an obligation at the entry level, because some mechanism must be developed to determine who possesses the competence and expertise to call themselves professional. If we believe there should be regulation of professional activity, then it must be done either by the government or by the professions themselves. The argument from expertise would say the preferable regulation would be by other professionals. If there is a need for regulation, and the thesis of this book is there may well be such a need in the area of providing unnecessary or excessive services, the profession must not only claim the power, but also must exercise it.

A second justification for professional autonomy, which would reach the individual, not just the profession, would be the argument in favor of laissez faire economic activity. Stated differently, this is an argument against the desirability of regulatory activity in general, particularly by the government. Licensing could be abolished, which would make the practice of the profession totally autonomous and break up professional monopolies. This would then make entry into the professions, like entry into other occupational categories, a matter of choice. Few people would be comfortable with permitting anyone to claim professional competence and thus be free to sell expertise in the market to anyone who would buy it. The standard counterargument to the claim that professional monopolies should be abolished is, "Would you want anyone to be able to hold himself out as a surgeon and perform operations even if he had never been to medical school?"

Leaving economic activity to the market does not mean it is unregulated, but rather that it is subject to market controls.[9] According to free market theory, the market works well to control price and supply, but there is little in the theory that deals with the dimension of quality. The standard neoclassical economic answer to this is that the consumer has the responsibility to obtain the information not only as to price, but as to quality. The problem, however, is that he must go to the professional to obtain the information he would need to evaluate the quality of the professional's performance, a situation that almost invites exploitation or fraud. Free market analysis assumes that the purveyor of goods or services enters the market for economic reasons, that is, to make a profit. This already slants the choice situation of the dilemma in favor of the horn of financial success. Nothing in laissez faire economic theory explains why a provider of services would or should forego obtaining a profit. Constraints on types of services that can be sold do not come from the market, but from governmental regulation, such as licensing, administrative controls such as the federal Food & Drug Administration's regulations, and the common law rules against fraud and deceptive selling activity. I would also add ethical controls. Many business people do forego making profits they could legally obtain for reasons we would label ethical.[10]

If one believes strongly in the value of professional autonomy, and I do, then ethical demands on professionals become stronger. Autonomy is valuable because freedom is valuable. It allows for diversity, experimentation, and risk taking. But freedom must be jealously protected. Its use must always be defended and defensible. The best defense is that the person exercising freedom acted responsibly and ethically. Notice that I did not say conventionally or cautiously. If the person to whom we grant freedom only acts the way the average professional would, there is little value or necessity for autonomy.

Although the professionals' dilemma can never be completely eliminated, there are ways in which the individual practitioner, faced on a daily basis with tough choices and judgment calls, can be helped. There is no single easy or clear solution, but there are a number of changes that would be useful.

First, there should be more complete guidelines developed in ethical codes. These must demand high levels of ethical conduct, but at the same time be flexible enough to set realistic expectations for typical practitioners. Some tolerance for good faith human error must be built into these guidelines, while at the same time, the expectation of best efforts to avoid harmful error must be retained. This development of good ethical guidelines is a task for the professions as entities.

Next, each practitioner must have a disposition or desire to comply with these guidelines. Cultivating this disposition is the responsibility of professional education and of professional modelling by the leaders of the profession.

Finally, the structures of professional practice must support this disposition to follow these guidelines. As far as possible, conflict of interest situations should be avoided. Competitive pressures from unethical competitors that make many practitioners feel they cannot afford to be too ethical must be minimized. Unethical professionals should be policed more strictly and the large financial rewards that might be gained from improper activity should be eliminated.

At the same time, we need to be cautious about overly strict and widespread supervision over all professionals, which could produce very cautious practice and excessive protective measures by ethical and competent professionals. Thus, it is a matter of drawing delicate balances or middle positions between extremes. But it has been understood at least since the time of Aristotle that identifying such middle ways is the task set for ethics.

In analyzing the problems and suggesting solutions, one's political and social orientation can play a major role. A favorite quote of mine on this issue is:

It is one of the critical instincts of the left to search out the institutional and systemic causes of oppression and repression. Political liberals will often blame individuals for social dislocations, as conservatives will usually accuse human nature. In politics as in medicine different diagnoses [lead] to different prescriptions. So conservatives will try to prevent change for which they believe people to be incapable, liberals will want to change the leaders, radicals must demand a structural reorganization of society's basic institutions.[11]

If we adopt a conservative stance, we could say that the drive to rationally improve one's material or economic position is so strong that ethical efforts to make professionals more altruistic and service-oriented are doomed because they run counter to basic human nature. Then we would be compelled to design institutions that will not permit this human nature to damage other people.

If we are liberals, our belief is that we can make people better. With a combination of eliminating some bad apples from the profession and of educating the remainder, we could then turn the next generation toward becoming the trustworthy and ethical professionals our aspirational ideals expect them to be. Most discussion about professional ethics starts from the liberal position.

Political radicals talk about structural change that would produce different motives and practices in professionals. My suspicion is that without substantial restructuring of the ways proafessionals operate as well as altering certain deeply held cultural attitudes, the problem will remain with us in essentially its present form. Whatever my preference, it is unlikely we will see the kind of social, cultural, and economic reforms that would eliminate the greedy self-interest displayed today by many professionals and other providers of services. The elimination of genuinely unethical professionals, the encouragement of independent advisors to clients, and a strong program of ethical education and supervision for the profession would seem to be as much improvement as one could expect.

A teacher in a professional school is obligated to walk a fine line created by the dilemma. In all honesty, I must recognize the enormous pressure created by the culture to be financially successful. Students and practitioners naturally have a strong self-interest in meeting this cultural expectation. The teacher has an ethical responsibility to present honestly the world in which her students must live and work and an equally strong ethical responsibility to be critical of the present reality to show ways in which it can be improved. If her perception is that the structures of society or of the professions are highly resistant to the kinds of changes she and many of her students feel ought to occur, to what extent is her moral obligation to help the students adjust and operate within social structures with which she is uncomfortable? Should she proselytize students to be ineffective and frustrated seekers after social change?[12]

The perspective selected may also be controlled by the position of the observer. If the dilemma is viewed from the position of the individual professional who is torn between the horns of the dilemma, then the current structure, professional values, and practices are givens within which she must operate. She can and should, as a member of the profession, work to change those structures and values she finds personally troubling, but until the change is made, they still represent the constraints within which she must operate. The dilemma is then an ongoing set of situational decisions that must be made by the practitioner. Formal professional ethics offers little or no assistance in deciding how to balance the two horns or the two goals of professional practice.

If our perspective is that of the profession as a whole, the dilemma is different. There is the appearance of formal high ideals and very questionable practices. This makes the profession look manipulative and hypocritical. One could approach this as a matter of public relations and try to persuade the public that the practices are not so bad and that most professionals are highly ethical. For this to be successful, the public must be persuaded that the ethical standards are seriously meant. Even more importantly, the individual practitioners must believe that ethics are to be taken seriously, since they are the transmitters of the message to their individual clients, both formally and by their actions. The public that is subjected to professional practices will form its own perception of the degree to which the profession lives up to the ethical standards. If the profession wants to maintain its prestige, autonomy, and control over its areas of expertise, it needs to worry about this public perception. The profession should be concerned with structural changes that will relieve some of the pressure on individual practitioners and will persuade the public that the ethical codes are not just self-serving public relations documents.

The liberal perspective may be justified on this problem and dilemma. Over the three decades I have taught in law schools, I have noticed that the only time I get undivided attention from the entire class is when an issue of professional ethics arises around some problem of professional judgment. Once this observation struck home, I began asking students about it privately and got a very common response. Most students would like to be decent, honorable professionals, but fear they cannot be successful unless they sacrifice their personal ethics and steer close to the line of sharp practice. They have succumbed to the cynicism of our age that assumes everyone is dishonest. It is not so much that this belief is used as a justification for acting unethically, that is, everyone does it, so it must be all right. Rather, they feel that acting sharply or unethically gives the others a competitive edge that decent people cannot overcome.

A task for professional schools and professional educators is to bring those assumptions out in the open and to test whether they are realistic or empirically true. If found to be untrue, our duty is to enlist all those professionals, students, and practitioners who wish it were not true to join in changing our operating assumptions.

NOTES

1. Karl Polanyi, *The Great Transformation* (Boston: Beacon Press, 1944, 1957), 154–56.

2. See Andrew Abbott, *The System of Professions: An Essay on the Division of Expert Labor* (Chicago: University of Chicago Press, 1988), 140, where he says:

> Some argue that the dominant professionals are oligarchs who divide the territory among themselves. They generally avoid each other's areas of endeavor and support one another against underlings and interlopers. Others feel that dominant professions compete like all professions and will fight each other if it proves rewarding or practicable. There is considerable evidence on both sides. Professions have in fact cooperated in a general defense of professional privileges against rising groups. But on the other hand, lawyers self-righteously pursue medical malpractice work, accountants fight lawyers over tax work, and bankers organized [sic] trust companies explicitly to take over legal work.

3. See discussion in Chapter 2.

4. This analysis, which counts the influence of various groups by their numbers, ignores the fact that professions, particularly the elite ones, enjoy well above average skills in manipulating public opinion and processes, unusually powerful connections with power elites, and great wealth.

5. When I was a recent law school graduate and engaged in practice in the late 1950s, such cooperation was more evident because there were

few medical malpractice actions being brought, and those that were were rarely successful.

6. In the 1970s, the American Medical Association organized a nationwide campaign to achieve major reforms in the tort system that they hoped would limit the explosion in malpractice judgments and the cost of malpractice insurance. Among the reforms were the introduction of screening panels to weed out unmeritorious claims, the provision for arbitration agreements to be executed between patients and health care providers, the grant of power to courts to review attorney's fees to ensure that they were reasonable, the abolition of the Collateral Source Rule and the fixing of a maximum dollar limit, usually ranging from $200,000 to $500,000, on recovery of nonpecuniary losses in malpractice actions (see Banks McDowell, "The Collateral Source Rule—The American Medical Association and Tort Reform," *Washburn Law Journal* 24 [1985]: 205). They had only limited success in persuading state legislatures to adopt these reforms.

7. The lawyer might say she is only interested in regulating the incompetent and negligent doctors, not those who are competent and ethical. If so, given the percentage of obstetricians and neurosurgeons who have been sued, competence would seem to be a rare commodity in those fields. The problem is in separating the one class from the other by reliable criteria short of a malpractice suit. Of course, the lawyers have opened up a regulatory option that is increasingly being used against their own profession.

8. It is an old commitment of the liberal political position that one cannot ask for freedom and autonomy for oneself without being willing to extend the same privileges to others.

9. See discussion in Banks McDowell, *Deregulation and Competition in the Insurance Industry* (Westport, Conn.: Quorum Books, 1989), 6–8.

10. See Stewart Macaulay, "Non-Contractual Relations in Business: A Preliminary Study," *American Sociological Review* 28 (1963): 55. This position is also developed in Ian Macneil, *The New Social Contract* (New Haven: Yale University Press, 1980).

11. Loren Baritz, ed., *The American Left: Radical Political Thought in the Twentieth Century* (New York: Basic Books, 1971), 57.

12. My struggles with this set of dilemmas as a young law teacher are presented in Banks McDowell, "The Dilemma of a (Law) Teacher," *Boston University Law Review* 52 (1972): 247.

Bibliography

Abbott, Andrew. *The System of Professions: An Essay on the Division of Expert Labor.* Chicago: University of Chicago Press, 1988.

Altman, Lawrence K. "The Proper Time to Tell Doctors What Will Be Expected of Them." *New York Times,* Oct. 3, 1989, 19.

American Association of University Professors. *Policy Documents & Reports,* 1984 Ed.

American Bar Association, *Model Code of Judicial Conduct for Federal Administrative Law Judges,* 1989.

———. *Model Code of Professional Responsibility,* 1980.

———. *Model Rules of Professional Conduct,* 1983, 1987.

Association of American Law Schools. *Memorandum 89–92,* 1989.

Baritz, Loren, ed. *The American Left: Radical Political Thought in the Twentieth Century.* New York: Basic Books, 1971.

Barron, James. "Unnecessary Surgery." *New York Times,* April 16, 1989, Section 6, Part 2, 25.

Bok, Sissela. *Lying: Moral Choice in Public and Private Life.* New York: Vintage Books, 1978.

Bresler, Fenton. "Thatcher vs. the British Legal System." *Los Angeles Times,* April 2, 1989, Opinion, Part 5, 2.

Clark, Eric. *The Want Makers: Lifting the Lid Off the World Advertising Industry: How They Make You Buy.* London: Hodder & Stoughton, 1988.

Cohn, Victor. "Doctors and Dollars: Is Greed Eroding Care?" *The Topeka Capital-Journal*, Nov. 18, 1989, B1.

Cowan, Alison Leigh. "S. & L. Backlash Against Accountants." *New York Times*, July 31, 1990.

Drinker, Henry S. *Legal Ethics*. New York: Columbia University Press, 1953.

Dworkin, Ronald. *Law's Empire*. Cambridge, Mass.: Harvard University Press, 1986.

————. *Taking Rights Seriously*. Cambridge, Mass.: Harvard University Press, 1978.

Ehrenrich, Barbara. *Fear of Falling: The Inner Life of the Middle Class*. New York: Pantheon Books, 1989.

Ellul, Jacques. *The Technological Society*. New York: Vintage Books, 1964.

Fowler, Elizabeth M. "Reducing the Stress on Lawyers." *New York Times*, Jan. 23, 1990, C17.

Freudenheim, Milt. "Health Insurers, to Reduce Losses, Blacklist Dozens of Occupations." *New York Times*, Feb. 5, 1990, A1.

Fuller, Lon L. *The Morality of Law*. New Haven: Yale University Press, 1964.

Fuller, Lon L., and William R. Perdue, Jr. "The Reliance Interest in Contract Damages." *Yale Law Journal* 46 (1936): 52.

Furrow, Barry R., Sandra H. Johnson, Timothy S. Jost and Robert L. Schwartz. *Health Law*. St. Paul: West Publishing Co., 1987.

Gorlin, Rena A., ed. *Codes of Professional Responsibility*. Washington, D.C.: Bureau of National Affairs, 1986.

Guggenberger, Bernd. *Das Menschenrecht Auf Irrtum*. Munich and Vienna: Carl Hanser Verlag, 1987.

Hart, H.L.A. "Positivism and the Separation of Law and Morals." *Harvard Law Review* 71 (1958): 593.

Havighurst, Harold C. *The Nature of Private Contract*. Littleton, Colo.: Fred B. Rothman & Co., 1981.

Hawver, Vickie Griffith. "Peer Review Agency Checks Care Quality, Costs." *The Topeka Capital-Journal*, Nov. 4, 1989, B1.

Heilbroner, Robert. *The Nature and Logic of Capitalism*. New York: W. W. Norton, 1985.

Holmes, Oliver Wendell, Jr. "The Path of the Law." *Harvard Law Review* 10 (1897): 457.

Keeton, Robert E., and Alan Widiss. *Insurance Law*. Student ed., St. Paul: West Publishing Co., 1988.

Kohn, Alfie. *No Contest: The Case Against Competition*. Boston: Houghton Mifflin Company, 1986.

Kolata, Gina. "Rate of Hysterectomies Puzzles Experts." *New York Times*, Sept. 20, 1988. C1.

Kultgen, John. *Ethics and Professionalism*. Philadelphia: University of Pennsylvania Press, 1988.

Labaton, Stephen. "Courts Rethinking Rule Intended to Slow Frivolous Lawsuits." *New York Times*, Sept. 14, 1990, B12.

Laut, Phil. *Money Is My Friend*. New York: Ivy Books, 1978, 1989.

Levine, Maurice, M.D. *Psychiatry and Ethics*. New York: George Braziller, 1972.

Lewis, Anthony. *Gideon's Trumpet*. New York: Random House, 1964.

Llewellyn, Karl. *The Common Law Tradition: Deciding Appeals*. Boston: Little, Brown & Co., 1960.

Macaulay, Stewart. "Non-Contractual Relations in Business: A Preliminary Study." *American Sociological Review* 28 (1963): 55.

McDowell, Banks. "The Audiences for Legal Scholarship." *Journal of Legal Education* 40 (1990): 261.

———. "The Collateral Source Rule—The American Medical Association and Tort Reform." *Washburn Law Journal* 24 (1985): 205.

———. *Deregulation and Competition in the Insurance Industry*. Westport, Conn.: Quorum Books, 1989.

———. "The Dilemma of a (Law) Teacher." *Boston University Law Review* 52 (1972): 247.

MacIntyre, Alasdair. *After Virtue*. Notre Dame, Ind.: University of Notre Dame Press, 1981.

Macneil, Ian. *The New Social Contract*. New Haven: Yale University Press, 1980.

"Many Nurses Say 30% of Operations Not Needed," *New York Times*, Feb. 19, 1981, C5.

Marriott, Michel. "College Tuition Costs for the Nation Increasing at a Reduced Pace." *New York Times*, Sept. 27, 1990, A13.

Martin, Barry S. "The Garrow Case Revisited: A Lesson for the Serial Murderer's Counsel." *Criminal Justice Journal* 9 (1987): 197.

Menninger, Karl. *Man Against Himself*. New York: Harcourt, Brace & World, 1938.

Miller, Anita. "Financial Planners." *The Topeka Capital-Journal*, Jan. 21, 1990, B1.

Morgan, Thomas D., and Ronald D. Rotunda, eds. *1989 Selected Standards on Professional Responsibility*. Westbury, N.Y.: Foundation Press, 1989.

Murphy, Bruce Allen. *Fortas: The Rise and Ruin of a Supreme Court Justice*. New York: William Morrow & Co., 1988.

1989 Fact Book on Higher Education.

Nozick, Robert. *Anarchy, State, and Utopia*. New York: Basic Books, 1974.

The Oxford English Dictionary. Vols. 2 and 3. Oxford: Clarendon Press, 1933, 1969.

Podhoretz, Norman. *Making It.* New York: Random House, 1967.

Polanyi, Karl. *The Great Transformation.* Boston: Beacon Press, 1944, 1957.

Prosser, William. *Handbook of the Law of Torts.* 4th ed. St. Paul: West Publishing Co., 1971.

The Random House Dictionary of the English Language, unabridged ed. New York: Random House, 1973.

Raphael, Frederick. "What Makes Norman Run." *New York Times Book Review,* Jan. 7, 1968, 4.

Rawls, John. *A Theory of Justice.* Cambridge, Mass.: Harvard University Press, 1971.

Rosenthal, Elizabeth. "Innovations Intensify Glut of Surgeons." *New York Times,* Nov. 7, 1989, B17.

Turow, Scott. *One L.* New York: Putnam, 1977.

Wolff, Robert Paul. *The Ideal of the University.* Boston: Beacon Press, 1969.

Index

About the Author

BANKS McDOWELL is Professor of Law at Washburn University School of Law. His previous books include *Deregulation and Competition in the Insurance Industry* (Quorum, 1989).